Alma Cogan

Alma Cogan

A Memoir

The candle burns at both ends,

It may not last the night,

But oh my foes,

And oh my friends,

It gives a lovely light.

Edna St Vincent Millay

SANDRA CARON

BLOOMSBURY

*This book is dedicated to
the memory of Fay and Mark Cogan,
my loving mother and father.*

Acknowledgements

My deep-felt thanks to everyone who shared their memories with me. Limited space has prevented me from including all that was so generously offered.

Thanks also to Caroline Taggart for editing and dispelling doubts; to Maryse Vassalo for her enthusiasm and picture editing; to David Blomfield for research; to everyone at BBC Radio 2 for their continued support; to Colin Morgan of *In Tune* magazine for research; to Roy Williams for a beautiful design and for stopping me from including hundreds more photos of uncles, aunts and cousins who were there when I needed them – Frances, Judy, Barry, Sylvia, Stanley, Patty, Linda and Ivor Silverstone, to name but a few; to Graham Curd for terrific art work; to Carole Finegold for her encouragement; to Rex Berry for his ideas; to Peder Johansson for the Swedish photos; to Chris White; to Barry Brown; and to Brian Greene for all his patience and understanding.

Thanks to photographers Terence Donovan, Harry Hammond, Angus McBean, Joe Waldorf, Roy Round, Howard Grey, Bruce Fleming, Michael Kirsch, Mark Sharratt and all the others whose work I've included; and to the following sources for permission to reproduce additional photos: Associated Press, the BBC, Camera Press, the *Daily Mail*, *Dagens Nyheter*, the Hulton-Deutsch Collection, Popperfoto, Reuters, Jack Brecon from Thames Television, Topham Picture Source and the Board of Trustees of the Victoria and Albert Museum.

Finally, thanks to Liz Calder and David Reynolds for being 'hands on' publishers, and to everyone else at Bloomsbury.

First published in Great Britain 1991
Bloomsbury Publishing Limited, 2 Soho Square, London W1V 5DE

Copyright © 1991 by Sandra Caron

The moral right of the author has been asserted

A CIP catalogue record for this book
is available from the British Library

ISBN 0-7475-0984-0

Designed by Bradbury and Williams
Typeset by Florencetype Ltd, Kewstoke, Avon
Printed by Butler and Tanner Ltd, Frome and London

Contents

Introduction   6

1 School and Tea Dances   8

2 Sussex Queen of Song   20

3 HMV Years   30

4 Take It From Here   39

5 Bell Bottom Blues   52

6 Minks and Duffle   69

7 The London Palladium   88

8 'We're Just Good Friends'   104

9 Around the World in Eighty Dresses   119

10 Name Dropping   139

11 Mrs Macogie Makes Sandwiches   158

12 Yesterday   175

Epilogue   188

Discography   190

Index   191

Introduction

$\mathcal{I}$N THE history of show business, I don't believe there has ever been a performer who enjoyed their career more thoroughly than my sister Alma. Her career of twelve years was short – as, indeed, was her life – but into those years she packed more enthusiasm and zest than anyone I've ever known. It was as though she were trying to live three or four lifetimes in one.

Not until recently have I been able to listen to Alma's records without being overcome by emotion. I can now enjoy them and appreciate the consummate artiste that she was. The 'laugh in her voice' wasn't faked, nor was it a deliberately adopted gimmick to sell records. It was simply the joy of performing that couldn't be suppressed in her, even after long hours in a recording studio searching for the perfection she believed she owed her public.

Grandma Cogan wearing the hat she didn't take back.

Our flat in Stafford Court, Kensington, became a meeting place for everyone in the public eye during the late '50s and early '60s. An incredible mix of people gathered there – not just actors and entertainers: the mix crossed all social barriers and included politicians and titled folk. Alma's endless work for charities, either singing or sitting on committees, brought her into contact with many of the lords and ladies of the day. The parties became famous. 'And at their centre,' writes Leslie Bricusse, 'shining like the sun, radiating love and warmth and humour as lavishly as she dispensed food and wine, the one and only, much-adored, Alma.'

Please don't skip over the family history to the glitzier chapters, for if you do you'll miss the time when Grandma Cogan, while on her way to deliver her home-made knishes for our Friday night dinner, stopped at Harrods to return a hat we had given her. Somehow in the exchange at the store the boxes got switched, and when Mum went to pop the knishes into the already warm oven, she turned to Grandma and said, 'What's the oven setting for a felt hat?' I still wonder how the saleslady at Harrods enjoyed the knishes.

I hope you enjoy this journey as much as I have. Lots of tears . . . but most of all, laughter.

1

School and Tea Dances

*I*N MANY ways ours was a typically warm, loving, hugging-and-kissing, outgoing and effusive immigrant family. Our dad was born in Russia, in Vinitza. His father, Phillip Kogin, was a tailor and his grandparents ran a small sweet factory. In the 1890s the Jews of Vinitza could either stay and face the pogroms or emigrate. Fortunately for us, Dad's family emigrated. In those days most European emigrants headed for America, but Dad's parents chose London and settled in Whitechapel, where tailoring was the traditional trade.

Phillip and Esther had six children: Mark (our dad), Debbie, Hettie, Harry, Alfred and Sammy. The boys were all trained as tailors, like their father. Life around their home in Davis Avenue was sociable and neighbourly – typical of the East End. There was very little money, but if there was a wedding, a funeral, a party, everyone in the street was there, and everyone sang, especially Dad and his brothers and sisters.

My mother came from a similar background. Her father, Herman Carp, had six elder brothers, who had all gone to America. He was headed there too. However, on the boat he met my grandmother, Gertrude, who, with her family, was emigrating to London. The two young people fell desperately in love, and because she could not bear to be parted from her family nor he from her, they settled in England.

Herman and Gertrude opened one shop in the Old Kent Road and another in Whitechapel. They had five children, Fay (our mum), Sarah, Beatrice, Rose and Alan. My mother, Fay, was very musical. She played the piano. Every week she would spend her pocket money on sixpenny sheet music. She played every popular song she could get hold of, and when she was only ten and the pianist at the local cinema fell ill, she was employed for a shilling a week to play music to accompany the silent films. Seated close up under the screen, with her neck cricked back so she could follow the action, she would play for hours on end, while her younger sisters, Sadie and Bea, took turns turning the pages and feeding her sandwiches.

That was the closest she ever came in her youth to the world of show business. In those days parents would never encourage a girl to enter so disreputable a career. She had the talent, but no opportunity. Opportunity would have to wait for another generation.

Our grandparents: Phillip Kogin (top), Herman Carp, Esther Kogin (left) and Gertrude Carp.

Mum and Dad met during a tea dance at the Café de Paris. Tea dances were one of the favourite forms of entertainment for young people during the late twenties. The most popular places in London for these social events were the Trocadero, the Astoria and, the best of all, the Café de Paris. Mum and my aunts would save their money and once a week, when the shops were closed for their half day, they would don their finery and transform themselves into glamorous flappers. So too did the Kogin girls. Aunt Hettie recalls, 'We would have dresses specially made for twelve pounds . . . always hand-beaded . . . with satin shoes dyed to match . . . and our hats were handmade as well.' I've always been told that when Dad saw Mum doing the Charleston in her crêpe de Chine chiffon, he lost his heart. He pursued her with the tenacity he brought to everything he did in his life, and Mum was swept off her feet.

Within a few months the entire Jewish community was buzzing with the news that the first-born of two immigrant families were to be joined in wedlock. The dressmakers were called in and everyone was busy designing what they hoped would be the outstanding outfit of the day. The wedding took place at the Heygate Synagogue in Walworth Road and the reception was held at the Portman Rooms in Baker Street. Mum's wedding gown was made of exquisite lace; the bridesmaids' dresses of

Mum and Dad on their honeymoon.

the finest satin. There were 300 guests, and it was the event of the year for everyone involved.

Soon after they married, Dad decided to abandon tailoring, move into the retail trade and sell ladies' clothes. It seemed a strange decision to his family at the time, but it was obviously the right one. Dad was one of nature's entrepreneurs. He did not like working for others. He always had to be in charge, make things happen.

Even our name had to have Dad's own stamp on it. His father and brothers spelt their name Kogin; so did their cousins who had gone to the USA. Dad had to be different. His shops were to be called Mark Cogan. So Cogan became our name, too.

Dad had style. He was always beautifully dressed, always

wore a stiff collar. He bought his hats from Lock's in St James's. His shoes were made to measure by Tricker's in Jermyn Street. He liked American cars, preferably Chryslers.

He was never short of money, yet he never became rich. The problem was that he was impatient. He seemed to be driven, a trait that Alma was to inherit. No sooner was a shop set up and running well than he would come home and announce to the family, 'We're moving. I've sold the business and bought another one.' These decisions made for a lively but very unpredictable life.

Mum and Dad were a remarkable team. She was just as strong a personality, but in a different, quieter way. Wherever Dad's impatient wanderings might lead us, it was Mum who decided on our schools and on the succession of starched and mostly forbidding nannies who were responsible for bringing us up. These nannies were essential in our home, as our parents spent all their working hours in the business. They believed their children had to have the best of everything and they were prepared to work for it.

There were three of us children: Ivor, Alma and – several years later – me. Ivor was born about eighteen months after Mum and Dad were married. Then came Alma Angela, two years later, on 19 May 1932, born while they were living in Golders Green.

Ivor and Alma were happy babies. Close in age and in spirit, they were good companions to each other, Ivor being very protective of Alma, very much the big brother. Alma once caused a major crisis when she dressed up in Mum's high-heeled shoes, for which she had a real passion, lost her balance and fell downstairs with a milk bottle in each hand. It was quite traumatic. She was cut to ribbons and had a scar on her forehead for years afterwards.

When I arrived, Ivor and Alma treated me a bit like a mechanical toy. Naturally, I enjoyed the attention, but it was probably more fun for them than it was for me when, not much more than a toddler, I was expected to curl myself into a ball so they could roll me down the hills in the park!

Mum and Dad's wedding.

At family gatherings, the singalong was the major attraction. It was at these get-togethers that Alma conquered all inhibitions. Everyone, especially Dad and his brothers, performed for this captive audience. Songs would be learned and prepared for the occasion. Alma fitted right in. By the time she was four, she was singing 'Begin the Beguine'. Even at that early age, it was apparent that she was a 'natural' with an unusual quality to her voice. It was against this background of approval and affection that Alma developed her love of performing. When I was old enough, it was taken for granted that I would sing too. Sometimes I was coaxed into singing 'As Time Goes By', but I preferred my pantomime act. I used to come out with a little stool, a clay pipe and a piece of string on the end of a stick, and sit there fishing. The family would have to sit there too, watching me, sometimes for ten minutes. It was so quiet you could hear a pin drop. I used to like that.

It was for all of us an unusual childhood, quite unlike anything we would see in our friends' homes. No children, I believe, were loved and doted on as we were by our parents. Yet not many children were expected to perform in the way we were: it was as much a part of our lives as brushing our teeth.

After I was born, Dad moved us first to Slough, as it was now wartime, and then to a large High Street shop in Reading, where we lived above the shop. His parents followed him there and set up a small tailoring shop with one of my uncles. This was typical of the way the family reacted to whatever Dad did. He was the one who led the pack. The problem for them was that Dad was always on the move. It was hard to keep up with him.

We stayed in Reading for some years. The bombs were dropping everywhere. We had moved to get away from London and the bombing, but the enemy had found Reading, too. Dad's shop windows were shattered more than once, but he had them repaired immediately and it never stopped him from opening the shop.

We still went on our yearly holidays to Torquay, where we stayed at the Imperial Hotel. Dad would drive us down and sit

Dad, immaculate as always.

on the beach with us in his suit and tie for the afternoon, then drive back to Reading and open the shop again next day. One time when we were in the hotel room after lunch, we heard terrible gunfire and, through the open window, actually saw a German aeroplane being shot down. Mum tried to cover us three children. It was quite frightening, as I remember. The plane came down on the beach right in front of the hotel. It was the talk of Torquay for weeks to come.

Our parents wanted to send us to the most conventional schools they could find. They insisted on private day-schools. Ivor went to a boys' preparatory school. Alma and I went to St Joseph's, a Roman Catholic convent.

Mum was convinced that because the nuns had no social life, they would be able to concentrate exclusively on the children. She may have been right, but there was only one other Jewish girl among the 500 pupils, and we had to stand outside the large hall in the mornings, while the other girls attended prayers.

One day at school, I was harassed in the playground.

'Why,' I asked Mum, 'are we different? Why do they keep asking me if I'm a Jew?'

The only answer to that was that we *were* Jews, we were to be proud of it and we had to learn to stand up for ourselves.

Ivor, Alma and I, of course, had no idea of how to do this. However, we had, on more than one occasion, seen our gentle, loving father transform himself before our eyes into a furious fighter. At the slightest hint of an anti-Semitic remark, he would not hesitate for a moment to respond verbally – or even physically, if sufficiently provoked. Once when we were out walking in the park, Ivor said, 'Where's Dad?' We turned around and there was our dad on the ground, on top of a man twice his size who had been foolhardy enough to mutter some offensive slur.

Despite our initial problems, we loved school. Alma was popular and clever, though not as precocious as I was, and we played our share of girlish pranks. At one time we even 'lost our hatbands' – the ultimate disgrace.

It was really my fault. Poor Alma was always expected to

keep an eye on her little sister. That meant dragging me around with her friends. One day we were having tea at Heal's department store. I was bored and put out my tongue at a lady sitting nearby. Next day we were summoned to Mother Superior's study.

'You will see three girls without their hatbands,' she announced at assembly. 'They are in disgrace. They may be expelled.' Alma and I were petrified; so Mum went into action. I have no idea what she said to Mother Superior, but whatever it was we got our hatbands back, though our friend Yvonne never did.

Despite the difference in religion, we were not really very different from our friends at school, except in the way we spent our leisure time. People still say to me, 'Did you go to Saturday morning movies when you were little?' We *never* went on Saturdays. We always went at night – almost every night. Our schoolfriends would see the children's films. We saw the grown-up films. In Reading, the Odeon was across the street from where we lived. The programmes changed twice a week and, as there were two films on each night, we would often go four times a week. I recently found a diary I kept as a little girl. At the age of six, I had written, 'Saw *Mildred Pierce* tonight. V. good. But Joan Crawford had too much lipstick on.'

Our parents were steeped in all things Hollywood. They wanted to see the films and, as the family did everything together, we saw them too. It was so much a part of their lives. Whether Dad saw himself as Jimmy Cagney or Edward G. Robinson, I don't know, but from his children's point of view, he did not have to go round acting like them; he *was* them. He had the profile of John Barrymore and the powerful, domineering personality of all those short, dapper, very forceful men.

We did not have television in those days. No one did. But when we moved to Worthing after the war, we would see every play and every pantomime that was performed at the Connaught Theatre there. We would also go to London to see Danny Kaye and Jack Benny at the Palladium. There was not one major star we missed, and we would always have front-row seats.

The house itself was always filled with music. My parents had a vast collection of records, from the Andrews Sisters to Al Jolson. They bought every seventy-eight that came out. We had stacks of them: June Christie, Margaret Whiting and all those wonderful band singers. We saw and heard only the best performers. That is where Alma's performance standards came from.

Those records were there for us to enjoy, but they were also for inspiration, and we children were the ones who were to be inspired. Mum and Dad wanted us to be able to perform, to do all the things they had never been able to do themselves. We were expected to become stars.

Only Ivor somehow managed to escape from our parents' ambitions for us. He learned the trumpet, but got asthma, and that was the end of that. Alma and I would not be let off so easily. There was no question of *whether* we were going to perform, only of how, when and where.

Alma and I had piano lessons, but neither of us played seriously and it was clear that we would never be as good as Mum. Off we went to dancing school where, extraordinarily, the owner of the school was taken to court for teaching children like myself to dance on their toes at the age of four. Luckily, before then we had learnt a lot that would prove very useful to us on stage later in our careers, but we were obviously not bound for the Royal Ballet. Dad bought me a saxophone and a drum set, and I was told to go into the basement and practise. I was only tiny then. I liked the drums and got quite a way on the saxophone, but I did not seem destined to be the next Charlie Parker.

What then of Alma? Well, Alma could sing.

She had had her first singing lessons at St Joseph's Convent in Reading. When she was ten, she sang at a Sunday charity concert at the Palace Theatre. Mum made her a special blue dress.

There was, of course, nothing unique about that. Other young girls sang in concerts, knew all the popular songs and

Alma, reluctant to be photographed for perhaps the only time in her life. The photo was taken by our uncle, Alf Grey, a professional photographer who took many pictures of us through the years.

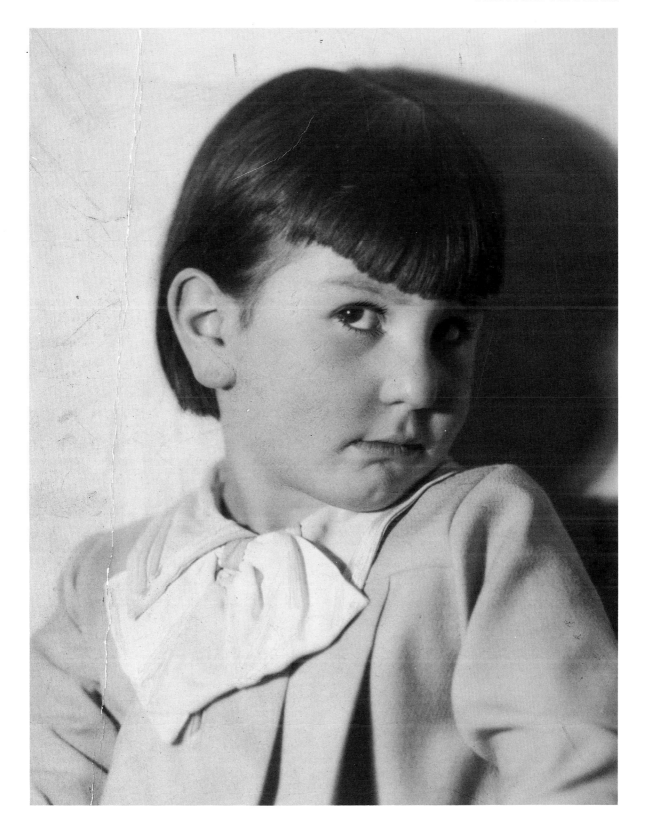

tried to sing them, too. However, there was something unique in the *way* Alma sang. Even then she had an extraordinarily deep, warm voice that was very mature for her years. Mum and Dad had heard enough good music to realize that she was capable of far more than charity concerts and family singsongs. All that was needed, they thought, was to find places for her to sing. Why not tea dances, the very setting in which Mum and Dad had met?

In the 1940s tea dances were still very much in fashion. For one shilling and sixpence you could have a sandwich, a small cake, a cup of tea and the chance to dance to one of the leading bands of the day. There would not usually be children there – unless the Cogans came.

When Alma was just eleven, Mum took her up to the West

Dad with Ivor, Alma and me.

End. She never forgot the scene. 'Mum persuading the band-leader, Van Straten, to let me sing with his band, and me a tall, frightened schoolgirl in my unbecoming brown gym-slip, sing-ing "The Man I Love".' Of course she remembered the gym-slip and the blue dress. Even at that age, clothes were very important to Alma and her ambition was to become a dress designer.

Mum and Dad, however, had very different plans for her, and Mum continued to take Alma round the tea-dance circuit, to cajole the bandleaders into letting her sing. Mum's efforts culminated in a meeting that, perhaps rightly, has always been credited with setting Alma on her way to stardom. It was in 1946. Alma was thirteen, and we were staying with Aunt Hettie in Blackpool. One evening they all went to the Tower Ball-room to listen to Ted Heath and his Music.

Ted Heath's was the most popular band of the day. They had a wonderful evening. Then just as they were getting ready to go home, Mum announced a change of plan: the rest of them were to wait while she and Alma went backstage to see Ted Heath.

With her customary *chutzpah*, Mum marched up to the great man and introduced herself. 'Mr Heath, my daughter is a very fine singer. Please listen to her.'

'I'm sorry, Mrs Cogan, I'm far too busy,' he said.

I don't know what my mother said to him that night, but it was like the time we got our hatbands back. Six weeks later, in London, Alma got her audition. As Alma put it, 'When I appeared for the audition he covered his face with one hand. Maybe he was concentrating. Maybe the sight of a thirteen-year-old singing "Prisoner of Love" was more than he could bear. He heard me out in silence. Then he said, "Come back in six years." '

'I thought she was too young,' Ted said many years later. 'It was one of my greatest mistakes.'

He did, however, give Alma some advice. 'Remember two things. First, when you sing a song you must mean every word of it. Next, you must always dress beautifully.'

Those few words had an enormous impact on Alma: she never forgot them.

2

Sussex Queen of Song

To TED HEATH, that audition was just another incident in a busy life, but to Mum and Dad it was a major triumph. Their dream of having their very own star in the family might now come true.

Alma knew that her role was to fulfil their dreams, but for the moment there were more immediate concerns. Dad had sold the Reading shop and moved business, home and family to Worthing. Our new house in Lansdowne Road was magnificent, just five minutes from the sea. It had a vast garden, and for the first time we each had our own bedroom. We were thrilled. Or, at least, Ivor and Alma were thrilled.

My feelings were a bit mixed. My room seemed so big that, at first, I felt quite alone. After sharing a room with Alma for as long as I could remember, I now had the company only of my little china animals. We were all very happy, though. Ivor now had room for his treasured Meccano sets and bare walls on which to hang pictures of the cars that were his passion. Alma was delighted to be able to set out her kidney-shaped dressing table, with all her personal things, and not be worried that little sister would be rummaging about. Around the dressing table she pasted pictures of the movie stars she so admired – Rita Hayworth, Susan Hayward and Ava Gardner – all cut out of *The Picturegoer* magazine. She would sit for hours in front of the mirror and copy their hairstyles, curling her thick black hair into almost any shape she wanted. To me, she seemed very grown up.

At school I gathered new friends and we were also enrolled immediately with the Pearl Hood Dancing School, which Alma begged to be excused from. She had discovered there was an art school nearby, which offered just the course she wanted in dress design and to which she rapidly transferred. She took every chance she got to sing with the local Worthing bands, particularly Wylie Price's Band. She would sing with them every Saturday night. They were not making a lot of money, so they were happy to have a 'guest star' who cost them nothing. Mum and Dad were pleased because they felt it would be good experience for her.

Alma and I used to hang around outside the Connaught, our local repertory theatre, in the hopes of meeting some of the cast. Alma did get to know one or two of them quite well, but there was never a date of any kind; Dad wouldn't have approved. Alma was offered a job painting the scenery, which, of course, was not what she had in mind. She declined. The next time she appeared there, in 1959, it was as a star.

Living in Worthing, we were close to Mum's parents. Their house in London had been bombed, so they had sold their shops and moved out to Brighton. Indomitably, they bought another house, where they stayed until their deaths in the 1950s.

They were a remarkable couple. Grandpa was quiet, but a man of exceptional determination. Grandma Carp was very much the matriarch. She was a forceful but wise and wonderful woman, with the memorable habit of expressing her opinions either in Yiddish or in English according to her mood, and occasionally, to make sure there were no doubts, in both languages successively. She called me Cinderella.

We went over to visit them every Sunday, and afterwards we'd do to the tea dances at Sherry's, where Alma would enter the talent competitions. One of these was for the 'Sussex Queen of Song'. At fourteen, Alma won that glamorous-sounding title, and it led indirectly to her first professional engagement.

At that time, only the youngest of Mum's sisters, Rosie, lived at home. Sadie was married to Leslie Lawrence, and they had one son, Ivan, who is now a QC and an MP. Aunt Bea and her husband, Gerry Dann, worked in a business that provided posters for most of the theatres in Brighton. There were five or

Alma and me outside our dancing school in Reading. I was a bluebird.

six theatres, including those on the two piers, which through summer seasons and pantomimes nurtured stars who were otherwise only heard on radio.

Uncle Gerry's friend Albert Rose was a bit of an entrepreneur and was looking for an opportunity to invest in the Brighton theatre world. In 1947, he became manager of the Grand, a fine, rather dilapidated Victorian theatre. It had been closed, opened and closed again time after time under a variety of names. Albert decided it was time for it to open once more.

One of his greatest coups was to persuade Max Miller to top the bill. 'The Cheeky Chappie' was one of the biggest variety stars of the day. As he lived nearby, he was happy to give the new venture a boost. It was up to Albert to find a supporting cast. He looked for local talent.

Uncle Gerry suggested he hear Alma sing. Wasn't she the latest 'Sussex Queen of Song'? Albert loved her.

He knew a lot about singing, and fortunately he also knew a lot of professional singers. One Saturday morning, while Alma was rehearsing the song 'I'll Make Up for Everything' on the stage of the theatre, a voice said, 'When you sing a number like that, dear, think of the story it tells.' To Alma's amazement, it was Vera Lynn.

'She sang it for me right then and there,' Alma told us that evening.

What Alma was not to know for years was that Albert had specifically asked Vera to come that day to confirm his hunch that Alma had real talent. Vera lived in Sussex, only about fifteen miles away, at Ditchling.

'Alma didn't even have to finish her first song,' Vera said, 'before I realized that here was a great prospect.' She urged Albert to give her a chance.

So, at the age of fifteen, Alma was engaged at the Grand for one week's appearance from 30 June 1947, on the same bill as the great Max Miller. What was more, she received the generous fee of thirty-five pounds.

This was the breakthrough that Mum and Dad had been waiting for, a *bona fide* professional engagement. They were

Alma aged about ten.

ecstatic. Alma was petrified. In the dressing room of the Grand, in a smart evening gown that added years to her age, waiting to go on stage for the first time, she was frozen with fright. The girl from the skating act was sharing the dressing room. She was ironing a skirt and humming softly to herself. Alma was amazed. How could she behave like that, when in a few minutes she would have the ordeal of facing an audience?

Dad had said, 'Just sing as you do in the kitchen and everything will be all right.' But this wasn't the kitchen. It was a big theatre packed with people. Suppose she lost her voice or forgot the words? Suppose they laughed at her or walked out?

Yet strangely, as soon as she started to sing, her nervousness vanished. As she warmed to her performance, she somehow sensed that the audience was doing the same. She felt that stardom might be just round the corner.

It wasn't, of course. The following week she was back at art school. Still, if she did not gain instant stardom and would not get such a fee again for many years, Alma did far better than most beginners. At that first performance she stopped the show, did an encore and took several curtain calls.

'Never mind about Max Miller,' the local papers said next day, 'there was a young girl in the show who is fantastic.' One paper even reproduced her birth certificate, as everyone thought she must be older than fifteen. After the show Max went to see Alma, to tell her how wonderful she was. True to his reputation for unselfish support of young talent, he even told the papers, 'You take notice of this young girl. I may have been top of the bill, but she will be next time.'

And she would indeed, many years later, come back to top the bill in Brighton.

Alma's luck continued. She next received help and encouragement from a local producer, Alan Crooks. He and his wife suggested that Alma should see Clarkson Rose, who was in Brighton auditioning for his show *Twinkle*. Alma applied for an audition and was offered a two-year contract at sixteen pounds a week for the first year and twenty pounds for the second. Delighted, she rushed home with the news.

'You're too young to go on tour,' said Dad.

'Out of the question!' said Mum.

There were tears and arguments, but they stood firm. They were convinced Alma would still succeed if she looked for work nearer home.

Frustrated, Alma applied for a job at yet another Brighton dance hall. Dennis Hale wanted a vocalist at the Aquarium. Alma beat twenty other singers for the job. That was fine by Mum and Dad. It was close at hand, professional and good training. Alma was pleased too, but after the heady week at the Grand, it seemed humdrum.

Then Alan Crooks brought news of something that was anything but humdrum: the Jack Hylton office was looking for singers for a new West End show, the Jule Styne–Sammy Cahn musical *High Button Shoes*. It was to open at the London Hippodrome and be directed by Robert Nesbit.

Dad reacted typically. Off they went to Jack Hylton's office.

'Sorry,' said the casting director, 'the show's cast.'

At that moment, a distraught little man rushed in and said, 'One of the contraltos has not turned up. What are we going to do?'

The casting director turned to Alma. 'What voice are you?'

'Contralto,' Dad answered.

She was rushed up to His Majesty's Theatre. An audition pianist was produced and she sang 'The Man I Love'. There was a long pause. Then a voice said, 'Right, thank you. You'll do.'

Dad said, 'I never doubted it for a minute.'

The pay of nine pounds a week was less than she'd had in Brighton, but this was London, and a major show at that. It was not the lowest pay, anyway. It was ten shillings more than the dancers received, one of whom was to be her special friend for the whole eight-month run of *High Button Shoes*. Her name was Audrey Hepburn.

Audrey, too, was almost new to the business, and the two girls would arrive at the Hippodrome hours before anyone else to get ready. Both were full of dreams and they spent hours together planning their careers.

In *High Button Shoes* Alma had a solo line: *I married a man of eighty. He counts his money and gets a thrill.* It wasn't much of a line, but she tried to sing it a different way every night – just to show how brilliant she was. 'There's bound to be some agent happening along who'll discover me,' she used to say. But nobody did.

Agents and producers may not have noticed her then, but it was thanks to *High Button Shoes* that they noticed her in the future. That show was really the turning point in her life, and the director, Robert Nesbit, was to take a big part in it later on. Until then, she had sung only because Mum and Dad wanted her to sing. She still expected to become a dress designer who sang for fun. Now she saw herself very differently: she was a singer who could design dresses when she was 'resting'. And Alma had no intention of spending her life resting if she could help it.

High Button Shoes did not just change Alma's life. It changed all of ours too: it was because of the show that Dad decided to move again.

At first, Dad would pick Alma up every evening at Worthing Station. He would never allow her to stay overnight in London. Still, as the show seemed likely to succeed, he made one of his lightning decisions. We were told that we were going to live in London. The Worthing shop was sold. A new flat was bought: No. 24 Stafford Court, Kensington High Street.

This time it was I who was upset by the move. I loved living by the sea and all my friends were in Worthing. Also, I had just taken the exams for secondary school and decided which school I was going to. Still, move we did – and, in my case, to a school that I was not at all sure I wanted to attend – at least until I discovered that Jean Simmons had been a star pupil there.

My new school was Aida Foster's, the prestigious theatrical academy of the day. I used to appear in pantomimes as an Aida Foster Babe and went on tour. I was always miserable going away, but Dad was proud; he had no qualms about letting me go, as the tours were very strictly chaperoned and we had

Mum, Alma and me on one of our weekly visits to Brighton.

tuition at the local school. I did enjoy, however, being in the film *The Belles of St Trinians*.

The end of term play there marked the only time in my life I was able to wear an article of Alma's clothing. The play was *The Merchant of Venice*. When the drama mistress announced the parts, I was certain that I would be cast as Portia. Instead, 'Sandra Cogan will play Shylock,' she said.

'Why?' I cried.

'Because you have the deepest voice.' The boys' voices had not broken yet.

Alma was persuaded to lend me her best New Look coat, which on me, because of the difference in our heights, dragged on the floor. It made the perfect Shylock cloak. The costume was completed with a false beard and Dad's *yarmulke* (skull cap). The family came to see the production and were very proud when I won prizes for both best actor and best actress! Alma said whenever she wore the coat afterwards, she felt like declaiming:

Alma in the 'Shylock' coat. It looks better on her than it did on me!

> If every ducat in six thousand ducats
> Were in six parts, and every part a ducat,
> I would not draw them; I would have my bond.

Ironically, only a few weeks after we had moved to London, *High Button Shoes* closed. That was in the summer of 1949 and for Alma there was a long, bleak spell before anything else turned up. She hounded the agents. She even took her turn in the dole queue for twenty-one shillings a week. The Labour Exchange where she drew this money was just a few yards from the London Palladium, where within seven years her name would be up in lights alongside that of Harry Secombe.

In desperation, Alma determined to crash into films, though not exactly at the most glamorous end of the market. She decided to get work as an extra. Ivor went with her, as he too was out of work. In case Mum and Dad would object, they did not tell them, but quietly went along and registered with the Film Artists' Association.

The very first day they were told to report to the White City Stadium for crowd work on the film *Blue Lamp*. What they had not been told was that they would be working on night scenes and that the session would last till eight o'clock next morning.

Once on the set they could not reach a phone, so Mum and Dad spent the whole night calling their friends, the police and the hospitals. They were frantic. Dad said to Mum, 'I just want to know they are all right – then I'll kill them.' When the 'actors' finally returned home, there was so much relief that they were forgiven.

The next film Alma worked on was *Dance Hall*, where she earned three guineas a day by dancing for the palais scenes to Geraldo's and, ironically, Ted Heath's bands. For three weeks on end she danced from seven in the morning until six at night. 'The dancing I loved,' she said, 'but no film director came rushing at me with a contract. I'd have loved that even more.'

Mum and Dad could see no future in this type of work. 'Honey,' Dad would say, 'I want you to be the tops. This is not the way to get there.' So back she went to the endless slog of endless auditions. 'Try your best,' he said. 'One of these days it'll pay off.'

'How could anyone fail with parents like that?' Alma once said to the press.

Then at last one of the auditions went her way. It was not for a show this time. She had decided to work up a cabaret act, and was auditioned by the proprietor of Selby's Restaurant in Hanover Street. She was given a two-week engagement. This was altogether a different kind of breakthrough.

Two weeks at Selby's gave Alma an entrée to a much more prestigious booking – three weeks at the Café Anglais, in the heart of the West End, in Leicester Square. Along with Quaglino's and the Café de Paris, it was one of the smartest restaurants in town. Our uncle, Alan Carr, had taken over as musical director there, succeeding the legendary band leader Harry Roy.

'Fay and Mark suggested that perhaps we might use Alma in cabaret, but I had to be neutral over taking her on,' he recalls.

Alma's first passport photo.

One of her earliest cabaret appearances, 1950.

'Our clientèle liked to see the regular people. We had Tommy Cooper, Benny Hill and Dick Emery – mostly comedians. They were not great stars then, but they were certainly experienced.

'For an audience like this, the cabaret had to be rather special. You were accepted – or not – in the first minute. Either they warmed to you or they would go back to their soup or, even worse, their conversation.'

So, for Alan, employing Alma was a gamble, especially as she was his niece, but from her very first song she got his customers on her side, and she kept them there for the whole of her three-week engagement.

However, she knew that the success she was after could only come through radio and records. That was where she must now look for the break she needed.

3

HMV Years

$\mathcal{J}$N 1950, Alma almost gave up her ambition to be a star. She had had such wonderful encouragement from her start in Brighton and the Café Anglais, but now it seemed that she was getting nowhere.

She told Mum and me years later that she'd given herself three years and a total of £500 to make the grade in show business. 'If I hadn't made it in that time, I was going to give up.'

That was her plan. She did not tell Dad, as he would never have accepted her giving up. As it was, money and time both nearly did run out before she made her name, and during those very trying years she often wondered if the promise was worth keeping. That she did so was a tribute to her tenacity and to the persistence of Walter Ridley, a producer at HMV records.

Walter and Alma were put in touch with one another in the spring of 1950 by the music publisher Joe Roncoroni. Joe had heard Alma sing and thought she should make records. 'Go and see Wally Ridley,' he said. 'He's the best producer around.' Alma told Dad what Joe had said, and an appointment was made.

Wally remembers the scene to this day. 'It was around lunchtime. Alma's father brought her along to see me at my office at the Abbey Road studios. The only studio available that day was the cavernous Number One studio, which they usually use for symphony orchestras.

'Alma sang "The Man I Love". When she finished, I said, "You don't really know what you are doing, do you?" I watched her closely. A remark of that kind to young singers could destroy them – but not Alma. She didn't flinch. And that was what I was looking for. I knew then that this girl would be a star. God had not only given her a voice. He had also given her character, a real inner strength, and I knew it there and then. With performers, character is vital. If they do not have the determination to survive, they are never going to make it.'

Alma kept the smile on her face. Neither Wally nor – even more importantly – Dad would see her disappointment.

Then Wally relented. 'There are some possibilities, though,' he said. He turned to Dad, 'I'll look after her, but only on two conditions. She has to tell me the truth and she has to have faith. If she doesn't tell the truth, we won't get anywhere, and she has to have faith, because she has to do it my way or I cannot help.'

Dad's reaction was equally unexpected. 'You do what you think best,' he said. 'I'll put her career in your hands: whatever you say goes, Mr Ridley.'

For Dad that was an extraordinary snap decision, quite out of character. Although Alma had by now been working in show business for almost four years, Dad was still very much in charge of both her career and her life. He had trusted no one else with either. Now he was effectively handing over all his ambitions for Alma to a man he had met less than half an hour before.

Yet perhaps Dad recognized in Wally something of his own background, something, too, of his own determination to succeed against all odds. By the time Alma arrived on his doorstep, Wally had already established a reputation for picking the singers and the songs, and the HMV label always got more than its share of hits. Still, he was a stern taskmaster, as Alma would learn.

'You have to get more experience,' he said. 'Get a job with a band. And you should also take singing lessons. Meanwhile, come to see me once a month.'

Alma was very upset. She had, naturally, hoped for immediate approval and a promise of a recording contract. Instead, she felt as though she were being sent back to school. Still, if that was what the man said, she would do it. For singing lessons,

Above: *Scouring the music publishers' offices for possible material.*

Opposite: *Singing for other people's suppers at the Cumberland Hotel.*

she went to Manilio di Veroli. I used to go with her – and wait outside, listening to her sing 'Finicule Finicula' hour after hour.

'Alma, can't you sing something more romantic, like "Almost Like Being in Love"?' I would say.

'I'm afraid not, Sandree' – as she always called me – 'Maestro Veroli says that there'll be plenty of time for those kind of songs later.'

Alma, like all young singers, would haunt the music publishers' offices in Denmark Street in search of new songs for her repertoire. She met Diana Coupland there one afternoon. Diana was singing at the Cumberland Hotel in the evenings, for dinner dances. She needed someone to deputize for her. This was perfect timing for Alma, and she was given a week's trial. Then, as Diana wanted to leave the job anyway, Alma was hired as a regular at twenty pounds a week. The engagement lasted for over eighteen months and gave her invaluable experience.

She sang from seven till eleven every night, and when she was not singing she would sit by herself behind the bandstand, learning new numbers. It was hard work, but she loved it.

When she started, she used to sing with what she herself later described as 'the most ghastly, phony American accent'. In those days, most singers felt that they could only be accepted if they sounded like the American stars. Joe Burns, the bandleader, tried hard to make her drop the accent.

'Every time you sing like that, I'll laugh at you,' he said. He did. And he cured her.

One of Alma's dearest treasures was thanks to Joe: a letter she received from a fan who expressed delight that 'you sound so British – not a copy of something from across the Atlantic.'

Every week, Alma went off to Abbey Road, where Wally Ridley would coach her through current popular songs that he thought were possible for her, or ones she had found on her trips to the publishers.

Such 'shopping trips' down Denmark Street were always good for Alma's spirits. They were fun. At the time I was still at school and in the evenings would return to be regaled with

stories of Alma's adventures.

On one occasion when she was visiting Michael Reine and Bill Cotton Junior, who ran a small but very lively business, they took her into the office to listen to a song. Bill remembers it as 'an awful place. We had a piano and a settee put-u-up which we had bought at a sale. We sent Ronnie, our assistant, out to buy some tea, pulled the bed open, and jokingly said, "Come on, this is our casting couch," when a huge rat jumped out.

'The three of us, with Alma last, were up on the desk in a flash. There was no thought of women and children first. There we were, all three of us, when Ronnie came back. He looked at us, and said, "I didn't realize it was going to be high tea." '

Alma swore she would never go back, but fortunately she did. Michael and Bill moved into new offices and eventually published three of the biggest hits Alma ever had – 'Bell Bottom Blues', 'I Can't Tell a Waltz from a Tango' and 'Never Do a Tango with an Eskimo'. Bill Cotton, the partner who had crouched with her on that desk, would become managing director of BBC Television, and a close friend in the days when cups of tea and rats in beds had been replaced by glamorous restaurants and elegant high-tech offices.

In those early days, however, none of the songs Alma found or that came across Wally's desk quite seemed the right one for her to record. Alma naturally became rather discouraged about her chances of ever making a record.

'Don't worry,' said Dad. 'Be patient. It will happen for you.'

Then suddenly she was asked to be the star attraction at a very fashionable night club. It was very flattering. She handed in her notice to the Cumberland and took the job. It was fun, but after a few weeks the manager suggested she should wear slinky gowns and do some sexy numbers. Alma politely explained that was not her style. She was then told, equally politely, that she should look elsewhere.

It was a shattering experience. Alma knew what it was like to fail auditions – all peformers go through that – but she had never been sacked before. Swallowing her pride, she asked Joe

Burns at the Cumberland if her old job was still available. Luckily, it was, and they wanted her back, so back she went.

Throughout this time, Dad himself invariably collected Alma at the end of the evening. He was very protective and wanted to keep an eye out for any men that might be showing interest in her. One of those was Peter Thompson, the Australian golf professional. He and Alma were getting to be quite fond of each other, but not to the point of planning marriage. 'With him going one way round the world and me the other, marriage would not have had a chance,' she said. She assured Dad it was nothing serious.

Then Dad dropped a bombshell.

We were, of course, used to Dad's sudden decisions: the sale of one shop, the purchase of another, the inevitable moving of homes. It was part of his restless nature. This time, though, we were all dumbfounded. We were emigrating to Canada!

Of course, where he was heading was America. That was what he had always wanted. I suppose it was what we had all been brought up to want. America was the end of the rainbow. In the 1950s, though, it was not easy to get American citizenship. However, Dad had discovered that we could emigrate to Canada and then move south. He had a close friend who had done exactly that.

We sold the flat. We went to have our chest X-rays. Dad sold his latest business. Unusually, this was a men's shop. It was in Surbiton, Surrey. I remember going there with him one day. It was a huge shop, with formal suits on racks. 'I don't care for it,' he said. 'It is not for me.' So he sold it.

Then, just as suddenly, he came home one day and said, 'We're not going.' There was no explanation.

Mum was very relieved. She had worked hard over the plans to move, but would have hated to leave the family. Ivor was really disappointed. He had always wanted to go and he had no job or girlfriend to keep him in England. I too would have liked to have gone – I had always seen myself working in the movies in Hollywood. Alma, though, was pleased to stay in London. She had started to feel that her efforts were beginning to pay off, that her career was on its way.

Hastily we got another flat. Mum hated it. It was a mansion flat in Gloucester Road, not her style at all. Mum liked modern architecture and modern fittings. So back we went to our beloved Stafford Court, this time to No. 44. No. 24 was not available.

And then, in April 1952, suddenly, shockingly, Dad died.

He was only forty-nine and had never been ill in his life. He simply woke up one day with a headache and died that evening at St George's Hospital of a cerebral haemorrhage.

Dad's death was devastating. I had never known anyone so full of life as he was. He had enough not just for himself but for all the family. We all seemed to exist solely as extensions of his personality. Now we were on our own. It was not just that we had lost someone we all adored. Not one of us, least of all my mother, had ever contemplated life without him. We did not know how we could face the future, or indeed what future there could be.

He had made no provision for his death. He was – and so was Alma – extremely superstitious. It was unlucky even to talk of death, and inconceivable to make provision for it. So there was no will, no insurance, no advice on what Mum might do.

What she did was typical of Mum. As we had no business, she immediately opened one. Through a friend, she found a dry cleaner's shop in Brixton, at that time very much a centre for actors and show folk. They were our most important customers. I was still at school, but I used to help on Saturdays, happy for the chance to talk to one or two theatricals, even if the subject was confined to spots on suits rather than on the stage. Alma was less pleased – she thought Mum should be at home, but realized that the business would keep Mum's mind off Dad. Mum ran it well – she would never have run anything inefficiently – and it brought in a little money, but it was not the world we were used to. We felt at a loss.

I continued training as an actress, as Dad would have wanted, and after a fortnight's break Alma went back to the Cumberland. Now more than ever she would persist with her career. Dad might have gone, but his spirit was very much with us.

I'm sure that Alma's biggest regret was that Dad did not see her name in lights. It was his greatest ambition and, by a grim sort of irony, after his death, things started happening almost at once. Fortunately, even if Dad had not left a will, he had left Alma a legacy – the promise that he had extracted from Wally – and it was on the point of paying off handsomely. Alma was preparing to make her first record. It was a ballad called 'To Be Worthy of You'.

Alma set off for the studio that morning with a degree of understandable apprehension. This was immediately dispelled by a good laugh when the receptionist informed her that the studio was booked for an exciting new young chap named Al McCogan.

In spite of that inauspicious start to the day, the recording went well, and some time later, with the record proudly clutched under his arm, Wally marched into the office of the BBC's most influential disc jockey, Jack Jackson. The record was put on the turntable. Wally watched Jack's face for a sign of approval. The song ended; Jack looked up and said, 'Smashing trumpet.' Wally was furious. Here he was trying to sell Alma, and all Jackson had spotted was a solo by trumpeter Jimmy Watson.

Jackson may have especially liked the trumpet, but he liked Alma and the tune as well. He played the record repeatedly on *Record Round Up*, and Alma was launched.

When Mum wasn't glued to the radio, listening to *Record Round Up*, she would want to play the record at home.

'Please not that one, Mum,' said Alma. 'It reminds me too much of Dad.'

The record sold well enough, but it was not a hit. So back Alma went to Wally, back to the practice, back to the singing of songs he thought might work.

It was at this time that Ivor dropped a bombshell of his own. He had decided to emigrate to America. We were distraught. We had just lost Dad – were we now going to be separated from

First recording: 'To Be Worthy of You', with Wally Ridley at the piano, trumpeter Jimmy Watson, and Frank Cordell on the right.

the only other man in the family? Mum pleaded. She wanted Ivor to be in the business with her. Alma and I suggested work in the theatrical area. Why not set up as an agent or music publisher? Alma had the contacts. He had flair. Our efforts were fruitless. Ivor was determined to go.

He went to Denver, Colorado, where we had close relatives. Mum's cousin, Lee Ruben, sponsored him. At first, his letters were cheery enough, but soon we had bad news. Ivor was in hospital. A vein in his leg was infected, brought on by frostbite.

Mum left immediately. Alma and I went into a decline. Apart from being worried about Ivor, we did not cope too well domestically. Mum had not prepared her two girls for this sort of emergency. As far as she was concerned, we did not need domestic skills. After all, we were in show business. Whenever I had showed interest in cooking she would say, 'Sandra, a kitchen is no place for a starlet.'

Mum had been away for about three months when Alma caught the flu. I was looking after her, when I seemed to go into a faint and ended up on the floor. At the time it was really frightening, but as usual it ended in laughter, as Alma decided the only way to pull me round was to throw a full glass of whisky in my face. It certainly worked, perhaps because it was the very first time I had ever tasted alcohol.

The doctor was called and told us that we were suffering from malnutrition.

That night Alma decided that we should have spaghetti. Two hours later we were still scraping it off the wall. Thank heaven, by then Ivor was on the way to recovery – though he would stay on in America for the next four years – and Mum could return before her other children faded away from starvation. Our cooking days were very definitely over.

4

Take It From Here

I T WAS Mum – as usual – who was right about 'To Be Worthy of You'. Thanks to Jack Jackson it was played often enough to catch the attention of at least one of the BBC radio producers, and in those days these were the men with clout.

The producer who happened to hear it and like it was Roy Speer. By a happy chance, he was looking for somebody for the series *Gently Bentley*. He invited Alma to Broadcasting House for a script reading in June 1952. She auditioned and was accepted. She was in.

Gently Bentley was not the biggest show on radio, but it was certainly popular. It was a vehicle for the Australian comedian Dick Bentley. He wanted someone who could add variety to his show by contributing at least one song and a line or two to his comedy routines.

The power of radio then was unique. Only a few people had TV sets, and even in the biggest of the Stoll Empires a singer could only sing to a few thousand at a time. *Everyone* listened to the radio. If you sang on a popular show you sang to millions every night. Alma now had entry into virtually every home in Britain.

She had, of course, made great efforts to get on to radio shows throughout her career. Over the years she had attended a total of four auditions, the first of them not long after her appearance at the Grand in Brighton. In every case the BBC panel had complimented her: 'A deep-voiced crooner showing *great* possibilities. . . . A Judy Garland-type voice, with very good diction,' they said. But they also said she must get more experience before she could appear on radio. Well, now she had the experience, had proved it in the way she sang 'To Be Worthy of You'.

Although Alma acted as her own manager, she accepted Kavanagh Productions' offer to handle her broadcasting contracts. This agency had been founded by Ted Kavanagh, who had made his name as scriptwriter for *ITMA*, the biggest and best of the wartime radio shows. Alma's contracts would be handled by April Young.

Almost immediately after Kavanagh Productions had taken Alma on, Radio Luxembourg, the BBC's rival, were asking if she could do an interview in August. The BBC agreed, so long as she sang only one song. It was the kind of compromise that the two giants of light broadcasting would grow used to making over Alma.

Rehearsing Gently Bentley. Left to right: *Dick Bentley, Alma, Frank Cordell, Josephine Crombie and producer Roy Speer.*

That series of *Gently Bentley* lasted for thirteen weeks. In October, Alma appeared in the BBC's *The Forces Show* with the ventriloquist Peter Brough, who then asked her to tour with his variety show. It was a terrific opportunity for her. If you were in Peter Brough's show, you were either a star or well on your way to becoming one. Alma was not well at the time – she was having trouble with her throat – but it was a chance she could not miss. Getting a release from the Cumberland, she opened well down the bill at the Manchester Hippodrome.

Peter was a big star and attracted big audiences. The show played the major Stoll Moss Empires at Chiswick, Newcastle and Finsbury Park. By Newcastle, the strain was taking its toll on Alma's voice and even Archie Andrews, Peter's famous dummy, offered to help her out. But at Finsbury Park there was no room for joking: she found herself unable to produce even one note. She needed medical help.

When she came home, Wally Ridley sent her to see a specialist, John Macmillan. He diagnosed laryngeal nodules. 'No operation can help you,' he said. 'You've got to keep utterly silent for three months, and then no singing for another three months. Even then I can't promise you that you'll ever be able to sing again.' Alma was paying for all the tension and unhappiness that had followed Dad's death.

Mum was appalled at this totally unexpected blow to Alma's hopes. It seemed so unfair. Wasn't Alma a non-smoker and teetotaller? She tried to make matters better by cooking Alma's favourite dishes and I assumed the rôle of Marcel Marceau, trying to cheer Alma up. We mimed to one another, while Alma dashed around the flat with paper and pencil at the ready, scattering messages like confetti. The infuriating thing was that she felt perfectly well. But she refused to let this strange régime get her down. She spent much of her time sketching in Holland Park, going to the cinema or playing cards.

Her career was on hold. She could do nothing but watch other singers go for the jobs she would have loved to have, make the records she knew were right for her. Yet in all that silent period of our lives – it seemed an eternity – there was one reassuring item of news. It came in a newspaper poll.

The *New Musical Express* had just been launched. It was owned by Maurice Kinn, later to become a good friend of Alma's. *NME* was a newspaper devoted to popular music, and it had introduced a poll for its readers to vote for the most popular performers of the year. Alma was number fifteen among the British girl singers. It was not a matter for headlines, but it was something to be there at all, especially when she wondered if she would ever sing again. Alma now knew she had a following. She had to get well.

She did indeed get well, much faster than the doctor expected. At the end of five months, he gave permission for her to start light vocalizing. Initially, Alma was terrified. It was so long since she had tried scales that she had lost confidence in her voice. But to her surprise she soon found herself singing with what appeared to be an increased range to her voice. In fact, she had simply rediscovered the range she had enjoyed before the nodules grew, but now she knew how to use it.

Alma and Wally set to work with renewed fervour to find the song that would put her on the charts. At that time, most of the emphasis in *New Musical Express* was on the American stars. Although there were good British singers recording at the time, such as Lita Roza, Cleo Laine and Dickie Valentine, few of them got into the Top Twelve disc chart that *NME* had just set up for the first time.

'Day after day we searched around to find something different, something a little more happy,' Wally recalls. 'Happiness was so obviously her style. Then one day when we were going through a couple of songs in the office, there was a soppy line that was all wrong. Alma and I had a fit of the giggles. We giggled and giggled, and then she went on singing – still giggling. I said, "Do that again." And she did.'

At last they had found what they had been looking for. As yet they hadn't found a song, but they had found something far more important. They had found a style – a style that was uniquely Alma Cogan. It was the giggle in the voice. It was distinctive – no one else sang like that. It also fitted Alma's personality and ebullient stage performances. It would become her hallmark and make her a recording star.

Alma and Wally's breakthrough was perfectly timed, as this style was exactly suited to the type of song that was to become identified with the 1950s – the novelty song. There was a growing trend for these up-beat, bouncy numbers that told a story. Alma and Wally might not have found the right one just yet, but now there would be plenty to choose from.

At this moment, the Grade Agency, one of the most prestigious and active agencies in London, offered Alma a contract. Leslie Grade was mostly responsible for the artists. His brother, Lew, who would become the head of ATV, handled production. Sidney Grace was specifically in charge of Alma's bookings. She was immediately offered a fourteen-week tour of the provinces with Richard Hearne's 'Mr Pastry Comes to Town'.

This was her biggest tour to date – and she now had to get used to walking out in front of an audience again, most of whom had never heard of her. Alma soon learned the trials of touring and Monday morning band calls. It was not easy packing and unpacking every week, but she was loving the work and it was on that tour that she started her nightly phone calls to see how Mum and I were faring, and to relate the news.

She earned a reputation for always being ready to do charity shows. She was asked to do one at Scarborough. Unfortunately, the Hearne show was then playing in Southport and there was no chance of her getting there in time by train. However, Alma knew that Winifred Atwell was in Blackpool and was also hoping to appear in the charity show. She did not know Winnie, who was already a big star. Still, she called Winnie and begged a lift in her car – and Winnie agreed.

'I don't know how I had the pluck to do it,' Alma said later. 'But I am so glad I did. When we left the theatre, the crowds all surged around Winnie for autographs and I just stood back and watched them all. When she finally stepped into the car beside me, I thought how exciting it must be to be a star like her.'

Later, they became very good friends. Winnie and her husband Lou were always up at the flat.

A few weeks later, when Alma was in Newcastle, she heard a rumour that Joy Nichols was leaving *Take It From Here* to go back to Australia and that the BBC were trying to find someone to replace her. Alma decided to apply.

We were all regular listeners to *TIFH*. It was by far the most popular comedy programme then on BBC radio. Its listeners were in the millions. The papers were in a fever of excitement over who would succeed Joy. Her rôle had involved comedy routines with her fellow stars, Jimmy Edwards and Dick Bentley, command of different dialects and at least one lively song to add variety to the mixture. She would not be easy to replace, yet the producer, Charles Maxwell, was flooded with applicants. Many of them were established stars. One or two were even male!

Against such competition Alma was an outsider. In the BBC she was known primarily as a singer of romantic ballads, with little experience of comedy and even less of dialect. Yet she had one great advantage. When she was on *Gently Bentley* she had often seen *TIFH* being recorded. She thought she knew what Charles Maxwell wanted and how he liked to work.

Her most immediate problem was that Richard Hearne's show was due to continue until October. How could she get back to London for an audition? At that moment, he suddenly announced that he must change his plans. The tour would be cut short, as he needed to rehearse for pantomime.

It was as though Fate had decided to intervene. She made a plan. The musical side would certainly be no problem. Her latest record, 'If I Had a Golden Umbrella', was exactly the kind of song that Charles Maxwell would like. In the weeks touring with Mr Pastry, she had been developing her flair for dialect and the confidence to tackle a speaking part. As for the comedy routines, her answer was to get herself a scriptwriter, practise a variety of dialects, hire a private recording studio and record it all. With the record in her arms, she went boldly up to see Charles Maxwell in the Aeolian Hall.

With June Whitfield when she and Alma both joined Take It From Here: *this photo appeared on the cover of* Illustrated *magazine.*

He was just going out to lunch and was surprised that Alma was applying for the job. Still, he took the record and said, 'I'll listen to it when I come back!'

'Up till then I had not thought of Alma for the role,' Charles said later, 'mainly because we were looking for someone who could do bright, peppy numbers, personality numbers, and I remembered her as a sultry, sexy singer from *Gently Bentley*. Also, of course, we wanted our leading lady to do what Joy Nichols had done so well for us for so long – play all the different character parts.

'Still, Alma assured me that she could do the lot and she impressed me with the record. Of more than fifty applicants, some of them big names, only Alma had taken the trouble to produce one. It contained some remarkably good character voices, too, and that song put across all the wonderful Cogan personality that we soon got to know so well.'

Next day Alma was telephoned and asked to come along for a script-reading session with Dick Bentley and Jimmy Edwards. It was the first time she had met the two *TIFH* stars together. It could have been an unnerving experience, but she had the advantage of having worked with Dick before and she soon found herself at ease.

Before long the list was reduced to two names: Alma and June Whitfield. Charles decided to hold a final audition, along with the scriptwriters, Frank Muir and Denis Norden. Unbeknown to Alma, Denis had already made up his mind. He had heard her sing some time before at the Cumberland: 'I'd been so struck by Alma singing over the clatter of cups and the serving of *hors d'oeuvres* that there was no competition. She was in from the word go. I knew, too, that her sense of humour was our sense of humour, and that she would *enjoy* being on the show.' The others agreed. On the other hand, June Whitfield was a very talented comedienne. In the end it was decided the girls were both so good that the best thing to do was to split the job in half. June was asked to do the character voices and Alma to be the singer.

The girls were sworn to secrecy, but it was clear they were

both in the running and newspaper columnists kept ringing up the flat. It was our first taste of press attention.

Alma was an immediate success. The first programme was recorded on 8 November 1953, in the Paris Cinema in Lower Regent Street, where she had first sung at an audition over six years before and been rejected. Now she was returning as a star, if a very nervous star.

Alma always hated first nights. She could never shake off an acute sense of anxiety. What was more, that night she had toothache. June remembers trembling like a jelly and being a little overawed by Alma's height and glamour.

'Jimmy Edwards clowned around the tip-up seats,' wrote Clifford Davis in his column in the *Sunday Mirror*. 'The photographers posed everyone for pictures. Alma's dark hair swished her shoulders as she looked down on the blonde little June. Discreetly Alma took off her shoes. Then someone said the pictures were to be full length.

'"Put your shoes on, Lucy," quipped Dick Bentley. Everyone smiled. The flashlights flared. Alma lined up with the comedians for her first read-through before the microphone. The big, blustering voice of Jimmy Edwards filled the place. Alma came in on cue. Writers Muir and Norden nodded. Producer Charles Maxwell sucked his pipe behind the glass of his control box – and smiled. The *TIFH* team were ready to get on with the really serious business of the evening.'

Although June was expected to do all the character work, Alma found herself helping out just occasionally here and there in addition to her singing.

For the new series, Frank and Denis developed a situation comedy that would come in the end to dominate the show. This was *The Glums*, with Jimmy as an appalling old tyrant of a father, Dick as Ron, his weak-minded son, and June as Ron's adoring fiancée, Eth. There was also Ma Glum, who lived forever in the background. All one ever heard of her were footsteps, a crash or an occasional shriek. She was Alma's responsibility. She had to go to the side of the stage, cover her

Overleaf: *The* TIFH *team: Jimmy Edwards, June, Alma and Dick Bentley.*

mouth with her hands and scream out, 'Whaddyawant?' or some other appropriate off-stage comment. For Alma, it was added fun and she loved being Ma Glum.

At this time she started doing interviews for magazines and newspapers and she was very busy. As she didn't yet have a secretary, Mum and I would do our best making the appointments, but sometimes she was double-booked. As Charles Maxwell remembers, 'She would get her appointments mixed up and sometimes arrive late, but she was so charming you could never get cross.'

He also remembers how thoughtful she was.

'When our first daughter was born, there was a newspaper strike. Alma knew that my wife and I were distressed that we could not put a notice in the papers to tell our friends. That week, for the one and only time, she insisted on introducing her own song. "I am dedicating this to our producer's new-born daughter, Sarah," she said. "It is 'Where Will the Baby's Dimple Be?'" Not just our friends, half Britain got the news.

'Over another strike she really saved the show. It was a musicians' strike, and at the last moment the orchestra and even the Keynotes singers decided that they could not perform. Quite unperturbed, Alma sang her song to her own accompaniment – of handclaps. The show went on.'

'One time,' Denis Norden recalls, 'we had to do *TIFH* in Bristol and we all went down in the train. The whole thing was a riot from start to finish. We stayed in a hotel with no heating and after the show we all crowded into Alma's bedroom and had a party. There were about six of us huddled under Alma's bedspread for warmth. Then at about one o'clock in the morning Alma decided to ring her mother to reassure her that all was all right. Heaven knows what Fay made of the noise in the background.'

Alma stayed with *TIFH* for three years. Ironically, she left it only because of her success elsewhere. It was an established policy that the show should have its own artists, who could be heard only on *Take It From Here*. Charles remembers, 'Alma, however, gradually became so popular as a singer that she appeared on a lot of other shows, and we all felt this was taking something away from *TIFH*. She was too big a star. Alma took the decision very well, but it was sad for us because she was a lovely person to work with. Happily, she went on from strength to strength; so for her it was the penalty of success, and a success that I like to think owed something to her time with us.'

Alma never forgot how much her friends in *Take It From Here* did to set her on her way.

1952: rehearsing for her first record. The photo was taken by Harry Hammond. 'It was the first picture I took of Alma,' he told me. 'I followed her whole career, taking hundreds of pictures of her.'

5

Bell Bottom Blues

ALMA'S FIRST appearance on *Take It From Here* came a
little too late to make any great impact on the *NME* poll
in December, but she did move up the list, from fifteenth to
eighth among the UK singers. As she had not at that time had a
single song on the record charts, it was a promising position,
especially as she and Wally Ridley had just spotted exactly the
right song to make the most of her new style. Alma had found
the place to launch it, too – on TV.

She had long dreamed of doing TV, and we had joked about
how handy it would be, just going along from Kensington to
the studio at nearby Shepherd's Bush. As it turned out, though,
her first appearance was televised from the Midlands.

However, before she even got to the Midlands, she had to
endure yet another of those BBC auditions. It was not enough
that she was now a star of *TIFH*. She must be formally passed
for TV. At least this time the man in charge was distinctly
familiar. It was Ronnie Waldman, now head of BBC Light
Entertainment. Ronnie, in one of her first radio auditions, back
in 1947, had asked her to 'come back in three years'. It was a lot
more than three years, but here she was.

When he moved from radio to TV, Ronnie had changed the
format of the auditions. He thought they would be more
realistic if they were conducted by a compère. This time he
thought he would try out a new compère as well: a young man
named David Jacobs, who was eager to move to TV.

David remembers that audition vividly: 'I knew and liked her
songs even then. What intrigued me was that for that audition
she chose a song that really wasn't in her basic repertoire. She

sang – quite beautifully – a very dramatic song by Noël Coward: "If Love Were All". Of course, that line of Noël Coward's, "A talent to amuse", really did sum her up perfectly. Fun was very much her business.'

Both David and Alma passed that audition and began their TV careers together. They found that they shared the same birthday, 19 May, and became very close friends. Through the years David has remained one of Alma's staunchest supporters, keeping her name alive by playing her records on his programme on BBC Radio 2 almost every week.

Alma's first appearance on TV was on a *Garrison Theatre* show for the navy, from Nuneaton, in February 1954. What better number to try on the boys in blue than her new song, 'Bell Bottom Blues'? She had a beautiful dress made with lots of petticoats. Bob Monkhouse was on the show with her.

'She was an enormous success,' he remembers. 'The troops loved her. They screamed for more. When I told the crowd, "Alma's dress isn't quite finished yet – it isn't easy sewing sequins on a marquee," I got my laugh okay, but Alma got an even bigger one when, after her first song, she twirled around and said, "I daren't keep still or the Boy Scouts will move in." The Cogan gowns were instant fodder for gags, and Alma loved to laugh at herself.'

Though it was found for her and published by her friend Bill Cotton, 'Bell Bottom Blues' was not an exclusive for Alma. Ted Heath was one of a number of people who had recorded it. Geoffrey Everitt of Radio Luxembourg was then reviewing records for *NME* and he quickly recognized that Alma had developed a distinctive style.

'She sounds like Alma Cogan and not like a dozen other singers. I'll take "Bell Bottom Blues" for a winner.'

He was proved right. Alma's was the only version to reach the charts. It was in the Top Twelve from 19 March to 28 April, at one stage going as high as number four. In all it sold over 100,000 copies. It was Alma's first big hit and made her name as a recording star. What was even more important was that it established for her a totally distinctive style. For the first time,

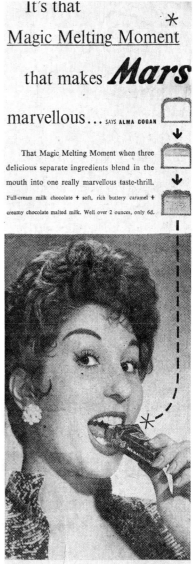

Alma was well enough known for advertisers to ask her to endorse their products – she got through a lot of Mars bars during this session.

Opposite: Sheet music sales were important to every singer's career.

Below: But Alma was beginning to have big record sales, too. In the Middle of the House *was a great favourite with children.*

people started calling her 'The Girl with the Laugh in her Voice'.

Alma was the first girl singer to become a major star on TV, and it is probably for her work on television that she is best remembered, yet when she stepped on the stage at Nuneaton, both she and TV were beginners. TV was, of course, only in black and white, there was only the one channel – BBC – but because of the broadcast of the Coronation the previous year, millions of people had rented or bought sets.

After the Coronation, television had to produce new types of shows that were different from radio and to find stars to suit the medium. In the spring of 1954, just after Alma's first TV triumph, two relatively unknown comedians from the variety theatre, Eric Morecambe and Ernie Wise, started their series *Running Wild*. Alma was asked to be their resident singer and began what was to be a close friendship.

Benny Hill and Bob Monkhouse also launched their own shows then, and Alma was first choice as singer for these, too. There she established another hallmark. Right from the beginning of her career she had designed her own dresses and even before the Nuneaton show had developed quite a reputation for gorgeous and outrageous gowns. For her first appearance on Bob Monkhouse's show, she designed an especially exotic creation with an enormous bouffant skirt. That evening everything seemed to go exactly right and the fan letters that poured in over the next few days all commented on her wonderful dress. From that moment on, Alma's dresses were an important part of her act.

With the pressure of *TIFH* recordings – she did twenty-six over that winter – things became hectic, but Alma amazingly never seemed to tire: she would tear through a sixteen-hour day of recordings, newspaper interviews and personal appearances plus her radio and TV work. She loved the business side just as much as the performing. She might well stay up until one or two in the morning and then be up again in time to be on the phone to Leslie Grade, who was always in his office at 6 a.m. By that time we had two telephone lines and seven telephones

in the flat. Leslie was a workaholic, just like Alma, and was the perfect agent for her.

Alma was exceptional in the showbiz world in that she had no personal manager. She handled all the detailed arrangements entirely on her own. She was constantly approached by managers who wanted to work for her, but she always declined. Her agents dealt with the contracts and the billing and she did the rest. Mum suggested a manager would lessen her workload, but she was adamant. It seemed she wanted to be in complete control of her career. When it came to business, she was Dad's daughter.

Her act, too, was very much of her own design, though she would always listen to advice. Every good performer listens to and learns from others, and Alma was a great listener, especially to those who had more experience than she did – like Max Bygraves. Alma first met Max in 1953 at Abbey Road; he was also with HMV. He came to see her soon afterwards at the Wood Green Empire.

'Why do you run on the stage and then run off as if you're in a hurry?' he asked. 'Never rush. You are a star.'

A star? She had never thought of herself like that before; after all, she was just a beginner – but she knew Max was right. That was how she had to see herself – as a star. She never hurried on stage again.

It took some time to learn how best to handle audiences. Half the battle on stage is knowing what to do when something goes wrong. I'll never forget the evening she was in the middle of singing 'I Believe' and everyone started laughing. She could not understand what was wrong until she sensed they were looking at her feet. She looked down to see her panties nestling around her ankles. The trouble with the hoop skirt was not being able to feel them as they fell down. She finished the number before picking them up and laughingly tossing them into the wings. 'If that ever happens again,' she said to me afterwards, 'I'll do it while I am still singing. I think the audience would find it funnier.' Her fans liked nothing better than the chance to laugh with her.

Alma was constantly on the alert for songs to record, and once I was inadvertently responsible for finding a winner for her. I had left theatrical school and would occasionally be asked to sing or do sketches for forces shows around the outskirts of London. These were organized by Dickie Dawson, a comedian who was a friend of the family. Dickie would eventually marry Diana Dors, but at that time he was always in and out of our flat. We used to treat him as a kind of older brother. He was happy to play the role, especially as he loved Mum; to him she was his surrogate mother.

At one of these shows I was doing impersonations, which

One of the most important people in Alma's career – dress designer Lily Anthony finishing off this very important dress.

were written by Dickie. Joe 'Mr Piano' Henderson played for me, which was something special in itself, as Joe was a rising star in his own right. After the show, Joe gave me a lift back to London. I invited him up to the flat for a drink.

With his usual enthusiasm, Joe went straight to the piano and played a new song he had heard called 'The Little Shoemaker'. Alma walked in as he was playing it.

She must have thought about it all night, because first thing next morning she was on the phone to Joe. 'Can I come down and hear that song again?' she asked. That afternoon she arranged to record it. That's how fast she worked. Incredibly, it became one of her best sellers.

Joe was already a friend and for the hectic summer months of 1954 he became her accompanist. For both of them it was a good experience. Joe was a brilliant pianist with a large following of his own, and yet even with his exacting standards he was impressed when Alma decided to record a new popular number called 'Little Things Mean a Lot'.

'Many singers would have run over it for twenty minutes to fix the key,' said Joe. 'Alma practised it for two hours, morning and afternoon, for three days.'

By the time the record was released, however, Joe had already come and gone as Alma's pianist. When he was free, he was there. When he was not, she had to accept whatever accompaniment could be rustled up for the show. But even when Joe was available, there were signs that he would not be free for much longer. An old friend from Brighton days would often be there, too, waiting in Alma's dressing room for Joe to come off stage: Petula Clark. Joe was about to become her pianist.

Pet's career ran almost exactly parallel with Alma's. They had first met at the Grand, in Brighton, where Pet appeared a few weeks after Alma as 'Britain's Premier Child Star'. (Pet was in fact only a year younger than Alma, but looked a child then, while Alma looked much older.) Now, though, they were both on their way to major stardom and there was no way that they could ever appear on the same bill, except for charity.

Alma and me in the flat. We were always messing around and taking pictures of ourselves.

Alma and Joe parted good friends, but she was left with a serious problem. She was beginning to move up the billing on the variety circuit, and on radio and TV. She needed not just a pianist, but a musical director. If Joe could not do it, who could?

With Joe gone she had to rely on whatever pianist might be available when she arrived at the theatre. Sometimes they were good. Sometimes they were awful. That was not the only problem either. The secret when touring was for your musical director to get to the theatre early for the band call and to hand out your band books ahead of the other performers'. If he did not do that you might have to wait for hours for rehearsal and then probably not have long enough to iron out any problems. Alma could not deal with all that on her own.

She was frantic. We sat around at home, thinking up names of pianists that she might approach. We went through all her

A more serious portrait of Alma and me.

programmes, while she called friends to see if they had any ideas. No one suitable seemed to be available.

Eventually she found the answer when listening to Cyril Stapleton's BBC Show Band one evening on the radio. The pianist, leader and arranger of the featured band was announced as Stan Foster.

Stan was well known in his own world as a talented musician and arranger. He had been musical director for the Merry Macks, an American singing group who were in all the Bob Hope/Bing Crosby 'Road' films. Alma could see immediately why the BBC had employed him. He was very good. 'That's the man I would love to have as my own musical director,' she told us, 'but obviously there is no chance so long as he is working for the BBC.'

About three weeks later she was booked to sing with the Cyril Stapleton band. There she met Stan. He remembers it well.

'My first impression was of a bouncy, very attractive young singer. I liked her voice. She was singing novelty songs and it was obvious that she had to plug her latest hits. Yet it was also obvious that she could sing any kind of song really well. We were introduced, went out to have some coffee.

'She told me she had a few weeks of theatre work coming up, round the seaside, and asked me if I'd be free then, as she would like me to be her pianist. My contract with the BBC only ran for eight weeks; so I decided to give it a go.'

At first Stan simply played for her as and when required, but within a few months she had so many engagements that he found himself working full time as her musical director. They would travel by train or car. The car was Stan's Rolls Bentley. The Rolls gave them space – Alma needed plenty of that for her dresses – and besides it gave them style. Even in the showbiz world, at that time, a Rolls was definitely posh.

In between appearances on tour, Alma would rush back and forth to London to record or appear on radio. In the meantime, her records were released at breakneck speed. In 1954 she had no fewer than eight, culminating with 'I Can't Tell a Waltz

Jack Hylton presents Alma to the Queen and the Duke of Edinburgh after her first appearance in a Royal Variety Performance at Blackpool, 13 April 1955.

from a Tango', the third of her hits to appear on the charts that year. She was now number three in the *NME* poll.

She did even better in a poll of the readers of the *Daily Mirror*. Here she was voted the most popular girl singer in the country and was presented with a statuette to mark the award at a concert at the Empress Hall. For Alma, that statuette was very special. It was the first of what was to become a treasure trove of trophies that she kept in a cabinet at the flat.

That year, 1955, was her 'Blackpool Year'. Blackpool was in many ways her lucky town. It was where she had first listened to Ted Heath as a teenager. Now she was to return to it, not ony to star for the first time in a big show, but also to meet the Queen.

The Royal Variety Performances were then and are still the most glamorous occasions in the world of variety. They owed most of their success to Bernard Delfont and Robert Nesbit. The shows are mostly associated with the Palladium, but in 1955 an extra Royal Variety Show was arranged earlier in the year in the north of England. It was to be at Blackpool, and Alma was invited to perform.

Mum was thrilled. To sing for the Queen was for Alma the greatest honour she had ever received. It was also nerve-racking.

What she did not know then was that such occasions could be just as nerve-racking for the organizers and for the Royal Family. The difficulty was that Royal Variety Performances always overran. Performers are not good timekeepers; nor are they used to performing for just ten minutes, and once they are on stage there is little that the producer can do to get them off if they go on too long.

The first of the northern shows, however, went well. The stars kept to their schedules. It was clear that the Queen would have time to stay on afterwards and meet a few of them, without any sense of hurry – though none of them had been told previously which of the stars would be presented.

Alma knew that she was less likely than most to get the chance. In such starry company as George Formby, Arthur Askey and the Crazy Gang, she was very much a newcomer.

Mum, Alma and me on our first trip to Paris. True innocents abroad, we were ripped off by a taxi driver and forced to spend a fortune on a visit to the Folies Bergères. We were staying at the super-luxurious George Cinq and had an orgy of shopping, so by the time we'd finished we couldn't pay the hotel bill. Fortunately, Danny Kaye was in town. Alma sent him an SOS and he bailed us out.

She had never topped a major bill. Naturally we had talked it over endlessly. Was 'The Naughty Lady of Shady Lane' the right kind of song to sing? Was it a little risqué? And what about her dress? Would it be perfect?

Even by 1955, Alma had built up a reputation for wearing exotic dresses, and this one had taken three months to make. On this occasion she was travelling by train rather than in Stan's car, and so determined was she that it should not be creased when she appeared before the Queen that she had wrapped it in a dust sheet and hung it from the luggage rack all the way from London, much to the amusement of the other passengers. It was a vast mauve crinoline with 14,000 beads on it and 200 yards of net in the skirt. She would scarcely be able to reach the royal hand.

It was not until the show was already halfway through that the word came: 'You're to be presented. Go to the pass door quickly after the final curtain.'

By curtain time, Alma was so worried by the thought of what the Queen might say that her dresser had to do an emergency repair job on her long gloves. She had chewed right through the fingers till they looked more like a pair of mittens!

She had no need to worry. The song went extremely well, and the first thing the Queen said was, 'What a lovely dress you are wearing, Miss Cogan.'

Alma breathed a sigh of relief. Then the Queen smiled and added, 'It's *my* dress I am worrying about. If we don't hurry up we will miss the train this evening, and I shall not have time to get home to change before opening Parliament!' Anthony Eden had just succeeded Churchill as Prime Minister, so it was a busy time for Her Majesty, too.

Alma was due to return to Blackpool for the summer season, but before she opened she had a triumph that almost rivalled her presentation to the Queen. She went back to Abbey Road to record a new song that she thought might do quite well. It was called 'Dreamboat'. It did better than quite well. In July it went to number one and stayed in the charts for fourteen weeks in all.

That summer Danny Kaye came to the Palladium. Danny had always been one of our very special heroes. When we were children Alma and I saw his first Palladium show; we used to sing his 'Lobby Song' at family singsongs; we were even convinced that we were almost certainly related. Didn't his family come from the same town in Russia as our family, and wasn't their name, Kaminsky, quite like Kogin? And didn't Grandma Kogin have red hair just like Danny's?

This time we did not only go to his show. We determinedly went backstage to meet him. Once there, we found his dressing room, quite naturally, crowded. For a time we hung around outside, trying to give the impression that we were really waiting for someone else. Generally Alma was the brave one who never hesitated to march in and introduce herself to people, but this time she lost her nerve and it was me who eventually pushed through the crowds and introduced us to our hero.

Alma and Danny became very close after that first meeting. He would call her from whatever part of the world he happened to be in and they would talk for hours. They didn't date in the conventional sense – their individual schedules didn't allow it – but they would attend charity functions together, which was their common interest. Danny would also invite Alma to his film premières.

I believe Alma was very much in love with Danny, more than she realized herself. He was the man she would have liked to marry, but he was already married and Alma was not one for breaking up homes. They remained soul-mates.

As always, Blackpool was awash with stars when Alma returned there: David Whitfield, Dickie Valentine and Joan Regan. Competition was hot, but the Opera House was the major venue and Alma was sharing billing with two top comedians: Jimmy Jewell and Ben Warris.

For the first time she not only sang, but also appeared in some of the sketches. The *NME* reported a sell-out, and its review explained why: 'Alma justifies her inclusion in the comedy

Introducing ourselves to our hero, Danny Kaye.

Alma and Danny – I think she was in love with him . . .

team, but it is her singing that makes her the most popular personality in the show. A warm friendliness and inspiring interpretation of Top Twenty titles captivated the two 3,000-strong audiences last Saturday.'

One night was exceptional. Mum was there and told me about it later. Alma had discovered, along with a large part of the audience, that Gracie Fields was in to see the show. Alma was especially good that night and the audience loved her. When she finished her show, she thanked the audience for receiving her so warmly . . . and then she said, 'Ladies and Gentlemen, this is a very special night for me and it will be for you as well. I want to introduce someone who has been an inspiration, not only to me and every other young singer, but to all of Great Britain. Mr Electrician, may we please have the house lights on, because I want to introduce England's first lady of song – Miss Gracie Fields.'

The audience, already worked up to a fever pitch by Alma's show, went wild – applauding and stomping their feet. Alma raised her arms to calm them down and suggested that 'with some encouragement from you, maybe Gracie will come up on stage and sing something for us.'

Gracie tried to decline, but she didn't have a chance. The combination of Alma's cajoling and the enthusiasm of the audience was overwhelming.

Would Alma feel upstaged? Mum wondered. Not at all. As Alma listened to Gracie singing 'Sally', tears ran down her cheeks. Her record 'Dreamboat' might be number one, and she might be a star of radio and TV, but she recognized this as something different, a warmth of popular affection that can only come with time.

That evening, when they were back at her hotel, Alma said, 'Mum, some day, I want to be like Gracie.'

6

Minks and Duffle

ALMA COULD never resist sending herself up at interviews and she often used to joke with journalists about her love of luxury. 'My tastes are very simple,' she would say. 'Only my ambition is extravagant – to buy two silver-blue mink coats! The first will be for my mother, the second for me.' This particular joke turned out to be a prediction. By 1956, Mum had her mink. By 1957, Alma had hers, too.

That was the way Alma liked to celebrate success. It was always shared, either with family or friends, and generally with both. Typically, she offered me a mink coat as well, but in those days I saw myself as a sort of 'beatnik' (most of my aunts and uncles saw me that way too) and I felt duffle, rather than fur, was more suited to my image as a serious actress. Besides, by that time I was making my own way and was getting a big kick out of doing my own shopping.

Minks and duffle coats! The Cogan lifestyle in those days must have seemed a little strange to our friends and neighbours. On the face of it, our flat, 44 Stafford Court, was conventional. So was all of Stafford Court. It was a block of modern service flats, which meant that it had porters on duty day and night, to greet visitors and to help residents shift furniture and luggage. There was an endless stream of visitors for No. 44 and, as for our furniture, it must have seemed to the porters that it went in and out almost as often as our guests.

The problem was that Alma, Mum and I all had different tastes. Other teenage girls decorated their rooms with pictures of pop stars; I went in for Jerry Lewis and Marcel Marceau. When it came to the living rooms, I liked the heavy mahogany

The first mink.

Top: *Alma's first car, a brand-new red Hudson Rambler imported from the US. It cost £1,800 – a fortune.*

Bottom: *Here it is again, parked outside the theatre.*

furniture of the 1930s that Mum and Dad had bought for the house in Worthing, where we had all been so happy. Alma only wanted modern – but Mum *loved* antiques.

Mum used to go to Portobello Road every Saturday and come home with a van literally filled with her purchases. As there was no room for them in the flat and the porters soon ran out of storage space as well, Mum would march down to Waring and Gillow, the department store that occupied the ground floor of the block. There she would buttonhole the manager and ask him to keep her antiques until she found space for them. She had such powers of persuasion that no one ever said no to her.

Bit by bit, our furniture began to take over the Waring and Gillow showrooms. Once when we were looking in through the windows she spotted a huge oriental bowl.

'That's nice, isn't it?' she said. 'I think I'll buy it.'

'Mum, you already have. It's ours!' I said.

Alma's bedroom was decorated in satin and lace, but the furniture she liked was essentially modern in style. Once when Mum was away we went to Liberty's and purchased a beautiful three-piece suite, two paintings and a rocking chair – Danish, in black wood. If we had to have modern furniture, I could live with that, I thought, but Mum hated it on sight. She thought the rocking chair had been bought for her. It had to go back. She hated the suite, too, because it was stuffed with down and she had to keep fluffing up the cushions. Even though we kept it for six months, Liberty's were somehow persuaded to take that back as well.

Alma won in the end, though. She bought an Italian dining suite. It was beige leather, very modern and very expensive. This time it was I who didn't like it, but I was away on tour when she got it and lost my right of veto. It stayed, because surprisingly Mum accepted it.

When Alma was not performing, it seemed as if she was always giving interviews. It was, of course, part of the work. If journalists wanted to ask her views on music, men or – their favourite subject – marriage, she was happy to oblige. Anyway, she liked people and loved to talk.

And so they all came, those columnists who were famous for covering the theatrical world, and those who were famous for being famous. As outsiders, and reporters of immense experience, perhaps they saw more clearly than I did myself the style Alma and the flat projected.

'In the sumptuous Cogan flat,' wrote Nancy Spain, 'we used pink napkins, drank out of red glasses and were lit pink, for rosy light poured on us through red-shaded lamps.

'A set of *Encyclopedia Britannica* stood lonely in the bookcase. The only other reading matter was on the backs of long-playing records, neat in record tidies. Voodoo dolls stood around. So did Spanish dancer dolls. All were well dusted, unconfused. Alma, chic in a black dress with a cowl collar and pink bedroom slippers, against her background of bull-fighter's red, looked like a sultry dark chrysanthemum. A portrait of her in a silver dress, hand on hip, dominated one wall.

'"Do you like it?" ' Alma said. "Painting is my hobby." '

Most of Alma's art-school work had been directed towards clothes design, but she loved to paint when she had the time, especially in water colours. The problem was that she had so little time to spare. The records, had Nancy looked at them more closely, reflected her taste, too. There was a major batch of big-band music by everyone from Ted Heath to Count Basie. Her favourite singers then were either friends like Frankie Vaughan and Vera Lynn, or international stars who would become friends later: Ella Fitzgerald, Frank Sinatra, Peggy Lee, Lena Horne, Mel Tormé.

In his turn, Godfrey Winn was struck 'by the clever way in which, so as to give height and space to the long room, Alma had kept most of the furniture on the low side. Despite its modernity, there was a Spanish flavour about the setting, because of the original idea my hostess had had of transforming a door leading to the hall into a grille of white tracery. Instead of a glimpse of the passage outside, you almost expected to see a fountain playing in a courtyard, and to hear nightingales singing in place of the

Stafford Court, showing the portrait of Alma by Fred Wood. I never did like the Italian leather furniture, but I was away when it arrived and lost my power of veto.

When the manufacturers made Alma a present of this bed, she sent it back by return!

Alma loved the 'business' part of show business, and was happy to spend an hour meeting fans in record departments (left) wherever she was appearing, or (above) to sign autographs after a show.

throbbing voice of Judy Garland on her latest LP.'

Another journalist, Maureen O'Hara, fell for the touches of luxury. 'Although she shares her flat with her family, it's her personality the furnishing reflects – and what it says about this particular bachelor girl is that she loves luxury. Nothing is allowed to stand in the way of her pursuit of comfort – when she couldn't find a low table big enough to take all the odds and ends she likes to have handy for her favourite seat on the settee, she designed one three foot square.'

I remember it well. We saw a table like that in the film *Designing Woman*, starring Lauren Bacall, and went out the next day to have a copy made for the living room.

'What intrigued me most, though,' said Maureen, 'was the number of photographs of Alma. '"That little lot is coming down tomorrow," Alma said.'

Those pictures went up and down like yo-yos. Mum liked our pictures up. Alma and I took them down.

Despite the calm, laid-back image given in such interviews, No. 44 buzzed with activity. Close though we were – and there are few families who could have been closer than the Cogans – Mum, Alma and myself behaved like three girlfriends, all of us with separate interests and distinctive daily schedules.

I was then at the start of my own career, which in those days involved anything from work on TV to appearing in night-club cabaret. I never knew when I would be in or out of the flat.

One day when I was doing a children's show for ITV, the phone rang. It was a reporter from the *Daily Express*. 'Can I speak to Sandra Cogan?' he said.

'Hold on just a minute, please,' I replied. I had wanted to change my name for some time, because I had always been known as 'Alma Cogan's sister'. I thought that this was the time to strike out on my own, but I had to think quickly. I had just seen Leslie Caron in the film *Gigi*. I decided then and there on my new name. 'This is Sandra Caron,' I said.

The following week when I knew the *Daily Express* was going to carry the piece about me, I ran out in great antici-pation. Here was my first interview. It started out by saying, 'A new star is on the horizon, Sandra Caron (sister of Alma Cogan). . . .' And that's the way it always was, and I learned to be very proud of it. Years later when I was on tour with Lynn Redgrave in *Billy Liar*, we were at the King's Theatre in Edinburgh when a fan called Elsie came into the dressing room.

'Oh, Miss Redgrave,' she said to Lynn, 'I do love your sister, Vanessa.' Then she turned to me and said, 'Miss Caron, I do love your sister, Leslie, too.'

In contrast to my unpredictable schedule, Alma was, of course, already a star with a carefully mapped-out programme that might require weeks away in hotels round the cities and seaside towns of Britain, interspersed with lightning visits back to London for recording or BBC commitments. She always knew where she would be, or at least where she ought to be. Usually it was away from home.

Mum would generally be the one at home, but not invariably. She might decide to spend a week or so wherever Alma was. I well remember my own twenty-first birthday. Both Mum and Alma were away. I spent it in the flat alone, feeling very sorry for myself. Still, I was working at Winston's, doing a comedy revue with Danny La Rue, and Mum and Alma made up for it when they came home, with lots of 'prezzies' and good stories.

When she was at home, though, Mum was, of all of us, the incorrigible nightbird. She loved gambling. She seemed to inherit the passion from Dad, as she only took it up after his death. Perhaps for her it was a compensation. At midnight, off she would go to the Victoria Sporting Club. In a bizarre reversal of roles, Alma and I would say to her, 'Now, don't be home late, Mum.' Sometimes, if either of us were appearing in the West End, we would stop off at the club and find her sitting there, with her mink stole, dark glasses and cheroot, intent on the roulette wheel. Sometimes we'd forget she was out and put the chain on the door, so when she came home at four in the morning, she couldn't get in.

It wasn't long before Mum's passion for gambling became compulsive. This led to many heated arguments – usually ending in tears – between her and Alma over the thousands of pounds lost at the tables. I often found myself in the role of peacemaker during those unhappy times.

Mum ran the flat to cope with our eccentric way of life. If Alma and I were both at home, and we would try to get her to cook, she was brilliant, like Grandma Carp. But most of the time she would send out to Jack Isow's restaurant for salt-beef sandwiches, especially if we had friends in for the evening. Sometimes I think we invented the take-away. Mum would certainly rather be sitting talking and being part of everything, than be in the kitchen cooking. Besides, she wanted to keep an eye on any man that might 'have designs' on her daughters. She had determinedly taken on from Dad the role of guardian, and none of our boyfriends had any chance of eliciting her support. It never occurred to Mum that we would want to be alone – or, if it did, she was having none of it.

The flat had four bedrooms, an office, a workroom, a dining room and the large lounge. Somehow we also fitted in a staff of four. We had two cleaning ladies – not because the flat needed two, but because Betty, who had been with us for ages and was like one of the family, hated getting up in the mornings. She figured that if Mum did not have to, why should she? As she never reached the flat till noon, we had Margaret, a delightful Irish lady, there as first shift from nine to twelve.

Betty had a little boy, Jimmy, whom she always brought with her, and a huge Alsatian dog, called Lassie, which she would bring as well. One day, bounding down the hall, Lassie knocked Mum flying just as she came out of her bedroom. Lassie was not invited back.

Betty seemed to spend more time in the lounge than in the kitchen. Whenever Alma and I brought men friends home, she would come and sit on the arm of the chair, and say, 'Ooh, 'e's nice, isn't 'e?' Betty was determined to marry us off.

She would then listen happily to our conversation, making encouraging remarks. 'Oh, Sandra, you are funny,' she would say. 'You should be on the stage.'

'I *am* on the stage,' I would retort, but somehow Betty could never get it into her head.

There was an Italian lady, Sylvia, who came in every day to do the sewing, and there was always sewing to be done. She did not work on Alma's stage dresses, which were made by Mrs Lily Anthony and later on, Raymond Ray. The Italian lady generally worked on Alma's day dresses, which were of a totally different style.

Alma's stage clothes were special. She had discovered that her fans loved glamour, so glamour is what she gave them: hundreds of yards of petticoat, flounces and feathers, with diamanté earrings to match. She would go off regularly to Mrs Anthony for fittings and to discuss with her designs for the latest of what Alma called her tea-cosies. (When she was on TV Alma would get hundreds of letters asking what she was going to wear next week, and what colour was last week's dress –

With fans at the flat. Jill Gates and her mother are on Alma's left.

black and white TV did not do those magnificent gowns justice.)

Lionel Blair told me of an incident that took place while he was staging and appearing on Alma's *Wednesday Startime* shows for ATV. 'I said to her, "Why don't you wear a plain, black dress for a change?" She thought that was a terrific idea and quickly had a beauty made up for the next show. Well, the viewers hated it! She got so many letters of complaint, she almost had to publicly apologize! They just loved those dresses, the ones she was known for. On one show I did with her, she wore eleven different dresses. Can you imagine? On one show? Eleven dresses!'

Much of Alma's spare time was spent on this wardrobe. She would have about eight evening dresses at any one time for use on stage. They would last only five or six months on tour. The dress she wore at the Royal Command Variety Show at Blackpool, for instance, was practical as well as glamorous. 'It cost £500, but when folded up in a trunk I can forget all about it,' she told her fans. 'It never shows a crease when I get it out again.'

People would tell her that she ought to look more sophisticated on stage. 'Rubbish,' she said. 'I think the gallery ought to have an eyeful as well as the stalls.'

Her fan club, under the leadership of Bill Badley, was about 4,000 strong. There were key members like Mrs Gates and her daughter Jill, Sylvia Kidderminster, Frieda Daiken and Bob Bluett. They would be in and out of the flat. Some followed her from show to show round Britain, becoming first familiar faces, then close friends. Sydney Sandbach, a devoted fan of Alma's, told me that when he was working at Brown's, the department store in Chester, Alma used to come in. 'She would give me a shopping list,' he said, 'and I would run around getting it all together for her. She was very grateful, as she was always so busy.' Sydney now has one of the largest collections of Alma memorabilia in the country. Others acted as officers of the club, liaising between Alma and the members, keeping them in touch with her plans. There would be offers of seats for her radio and TV shows, chances to attend *Juke Box Jury* perhaps, or *Ready Steady Go*, and on one famous occasion, the opportunity to appear on a record.

The song was 'We Got Love'. Alma had decided she wanted a live accompaniment, so she threw a party for several hundred of the fans and then set out for Abbey Road – 'like the Pied Piper', as she said – followed by the members of this new backing group. There, under Stan Foster's discipline, they were transformed into ladies and gentlemen of the chorus. The studio staff were astounded, but to Alma and the fans this was really no more than business as usual. After all, it happened in her shows all the time. 'Come on, let's hear you,' she would cry. The only difference was that this time they would get the chance to hear themselves, on record.

Usually it was her hairstyle, her dresses and her fabled treasure trove of 500 pairs of earrings that the fans seemed most interested in. They were essential parts of her public personality. Girls would ask their hairdressers to 'make it look like Alma'.

Stewart Hiscock, Alma's hairdresser and our friend all through the years, remembers lots of last-minute hitches. 'She was off to a première and I was to go with her. Her car hadn't arrived, so I ran out into Kensington High Street and hailed a cab. As Alma's dress had arrived only minutes before, the hem was not quite finished, so there I was on the floor of the cab in my dinner suit trying to sew it up. We came to a stop light and a tourist coach pulled up beside us. We must have presented quite a sight.'

Sometimes organizations would write and ask Alma to give them dresses to auction. This was not too easy, as after she had worn them once or twice nightly for some months, there was not an awful lot left to auction.

There was even one occasion when there was not much left to cover Alma! She was doing a one-nighter in the Isle of Man and visiting Aunt Hettie and Uncle Alf, who were living there at the time. Their son, Howard Gray, is now a well-known photographer and took a number of the pictures in this book. Uncle Alf remembers Alma's visit vividly:

'The show was a great success, and for once she took the risk

The famous dresses.

Left: *This one made its debut on an ATV show. It had 12,964 diamanté beads and seven skirts and needed two men to carry it.*
Right: *The sequins often caused problems for the early TV cameras.*
Below: *This was ice-blue satin, and one of four Alma took on tour. Between them, they were worth £2,000 – and that was in 1959!*

Left: *There were 250 yards of net in this petticoat.*
Right: *In the 1960s, Alma lost weight and adopted a fashionable beehive hairstyle, but she still loved her feathers.*

of leaving the theatre in her stage dress. I have never seen anything like the crush outside. She had this beautiful green dress with feathers all over it and by the time I got her into the car, she did not have a feather left. It was like plucking a chicken. She wasn't really disturbed by it and they didn't hurt her, but there must have been 2,000 fans there and not a single bodyguard.'

Of course there was no bodyguard. That was not her style and the Douglas incident was hardly typical. The fans were generally very well behaved and remarkably generous, too. Alma would get hundreds of presents, ranging from earrings to silver tea-sets, cut glass and thousands of cards.

She had a reputation for answering her fan mail personally and somehow she got through it all, aided by her secretary. She had several secretaries over the years and the one that stayed longest and that we had a good time with was Sue, a young deb who was 'coming out that season'. Our household must have seemed very unusual to her. 'Oh, Sandra,' she would say, 'you are so lucky to be able to have breakfast in your dressing gown. Daddy never allows me to.'

In all, some hundreds of letters would pass through the Cogan letter box every day, from all over the world. Most fans asked for autographed photos. Others wanted brooches, hand-kerchiefs, even lipstick kisses on shirt collars! There were a lot of manuscripts from up-and-coming songwriters – 'More Than Ever Now', a song which Alma recorded in 1955, came through the post. Some teenagers would write and ask Alma to design dresses for them for special occasions such as weddings. Somehow she would always find a few minutes to settle down and sketch out some appropriate pattern. In her time she must have designed dresses for hundreds of her fans.

The fans would ask for advice, too, if they were planning a stage career. She tried to help as much as she could without being negative. Her advice reflected her own experience and her particular view of show business.

'At auditions, always sing a standard rather than the latest hit which the producers have just heard over and over again. And dress to make your audience notice you. Learn from the film spectaculars. Their directors make sure that there is plenty of glamour for the eyes to feast on: gorgeous dresses, sweeping trains, colour, colour all the way.

'If you want to get ahead, accept any job you are offered. The experience will always be valuable. And be prepared to work fifteen to sixteen hours every day.'

I would often come home to find her at work autographing photographs and planning her responses to yet another batch of letters. The more she travelled, the more mail she received. She would push some of the letters across to me to read.

With the fan mail. One Christmas there was so much of it we couldn't open the door to the flat.

Some were brief and to the point: 'Dear Alma Cogan. I think you are smashing.' A seven-year-old, I would guess from the penmanship – and from the smudges! There was always a pile of letters from schoolchildren, and from families. There was something about Alma's style that appealed right across the age range. She even had admiring letters from female impersonators.

The forces' favourite.

There were usually some from servicemen as well. 'We are all fans of yours out here. Whenever we hear your unmistakable voice there is always a yell for silence in the billet.' From the days when she first launched 'Bell Bottom Blues' on that naval audience in 1954, Alma had become in many ways Vera Lynn's natural successor as uncrowned 'Forces Favourite', making special trips to entertain the troops round Britain and abroad.

Answering letters like those posed no problems. Others, though, Alma found it difficult to respond to. What do you reply to a pathetic little note that says, 'I cry myself to sleep at night because I can't meet you'? That needed more than the usual quick letter of thanks and a signed photograph. Alma would have to arrange for something special.

Life in the flat was like a merry-go-round. There were so many people. It was like one of those movies from the Twenties or Thirties, when everyone is rushing in and out of a flat. Only late at night – unless Alma decided to have a party – was there any chance to relax. Then we would sit around in our dressing gowns, sipping hot milk and talking over the day's happenings. Most of this would be girl talk or discussions about one of our latest performances. Just occasionally, though, one of those performances would be extraordinary – like the time Alma was asked to entertain at a staff ball. She did not often do staff balls, but this was very special. It was at Windsor Castle.

When Alma came home, Mum and I were sitting in the lounge. 'What was it like? Did you see the Queen?' We bombarded her with questions.

Alma sighed. 'It was terribly dull! The Royal Family didn't even show up.'

Then we caught the twinkle in her eye and she told us what had really happened. The Queen and the Duke of Edinburgh were both there – all the time. After she had sung her songs, she was presented and they all went into the ballroom. The band struck up with the 'Palais Glide'.

The Queen asked her, 'Do you know this dance, Miss Cogan?'

Alma admitted she had never heard of it. The Queen smiled. 'The Duke and I will teach you. Come along.'

'Oh, Mum!' Alma's eyes shone. 'There I was dancing round the room with one arm round the Queen's waist and the other round the Duke of Edinburgh's. If only Dad could have seen me!'

Alma really missed Dad. We all did, especially when we were together at home like that. He was the one who wanted Alma's success more than anyone, yet he was the one who never saw it. Alma, in a sense, never stopped performing for him.

7

The London Palladium

In panto. Alma was always ready to laugh at herself, and panto was a perfect vehicle for her clowning.

7HE DREAM of every performer in the 1950s was to appear at the London Palladium. The seed of Alma's ambition to sing on that stage must have been planted in the days when Dad would take us all to see the great international artistes. The headliners were often the American stars like Jack Benny, Burns and Allen, Danny Kaye, Sophie Tucker and all our other idols who came across the sea. They would frequently say that the London Palladium was more important to them than an engagement at the Palace in New York and that the highlight for them would be an appearance there before the Queen in a Royal Variety Performance. For our family, sitting next to each other, watching those outstanding performers was almost a religious experience.

Alma's own first appearance at the Palladium was in October 1955, in the ATV series *Sunday Night at the London Palladium*, compèred by Bruce Forsyth. Bruce tells it like this: 'Alma was the first British singer to be featured in the show. She appeared three times that autumn. I loved introducing her. We would chat a bit – we had this terrific rapport on stage, as well as off. I had met her first at Blackpool. We were both doing summer seasons. When you're there five months, you get to spend quite a bit of time together.'

Alma loved pantomimes. Her first was *Aladdin*, with Dave King, at the Chiswick Empire. Her role was built into the plot as part of the celebrations after Aladdin's escape. Aladdin would rub his lamp and the genie would say, 'If you had one wish, Master, what would it be?' Aladdin would reply, 'To have Alma Cogan appear and sing to me.' And as if by magic, from a huge puff of smoke, she would appear. It might have seemed corny, but the audience loved it and so did she.

She was a guest star in several more pantos over the years, one of them even taking her on a nostalgic trip back to Worthing, to play at the Connaught. Her only objection was that she found them time-consuming, which is one of the reasons why she never went into a musical in the West End. She really was not interested in a long run of any kind, feeling that it would interfere with her TV and recording career. Besides, what she loved most was the direct contact with an audience she got in a personal appearance, as opposed to doing theatre, where the tradition of the 'fourth wall' is observed.

She was offered scripts, of course. On one occasion the producer of *The Pajama Game* was looking for a new leading lady, when he heard Alma singing one evening on his car radio. He immediately cabled his colleagues in New York to say he had found the girl. He then went to see Alma. She asked to see the script. Two days later she rang and declined the part.

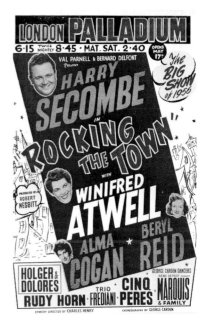

Rocking the Town gave Alma her first season at the Palladium. She had arrived!

The producer was amazed. *The Pajama Game* was the biggest show in London. 'What is wrong with it?' he asked.

'It's a lovely show,' Alma replied, 'but the whole is bigger than the parts. In my part there's not a single song that stops the show.'

Sometimes I found her decisions baffling. A career in theatre was what I was planning for myself, and here she was turning down lead roles. Still, her choices always seemed to turn out right for her.

In 1956, she had another four records on the charts: 'Willie Can', 'The Birds and the Bees', 'Why Do Fools Fall in Love?' and 'In the Middle of the House'. Then, in March, Val Parnell presented a show at the Palladium which for the very first time featured exclusively British recording stars. It was called *The London Palladium's Record Star Show*. The compère was Tommy Trinder and it was a huge success.

A mere four months later, Bernard Delfont and Robert Nesbit produced *Rocking the Town*. They invited Alma and Winifred Atwell back from the March show to star with Harry

Secombe and Beryl Reid. Alma could hardly believe that she had been invited back after such a short time. Mum immediately began to have a dress made for the opening.

Robert Nesbit recalls: 'It was one of the most lavish and expensive shows we had ever done at the Palladium. Alma was marvellous, appearing in production numbers as well as her own act. When the curtain went up at the opening Alma was on stage doing a number called "Rocking the Town". There were three drummers with her on stage and a full orchestra in the pit – very exciting. Later in the show, because "Dreamboat" had been such a big hit for her and so many people had seen her do it during her personal appearances and on TV, I wanted to do

A fan's snapshot in a dressing room.

something especially different; so I used the revolving stage, with walls and special lighting. It was all very glamorous and romantic.'

Alma felt herself fortunate to be working with Bernard and Robert, two of her favourite people, especially as Robert had directed Alma many years before – in *High Button Shoes* – and would direct her in many more shows, becoming a close friend of the family. They were both brilliant and knowledgeable

*Harry Secombe and Beryl Reid
help Alma celebrate her twenty-
fourth birthday at the Palladium.*

Friday, November 23, 1956

HOW NME READERS

OUTSTANDING BRITISH FEMININE
SINGER

1.	ALMA COGAN	9,466
2.	Lita Roza	8,241
3.	Anne Shelton	5,702
4.	Ruby Murray	5,418
5.	Edna Savage	4,634
6.	Joan Regan	4,627
7.	Eve Boswell	2,436
8.	Vera Lynn	2,305
9.	Cleo Laine	1,802
10.	Petula Clark	1,793
11.	Yana	1,339
12.	Patti Lewis	1,130
13.	Marion Ryan	1,004
13.	Shirley Bassey	1,004
15.	Rose Brennan	861
16.	Janie Marden	789
17.	Billie Anthony	464
18.	Ottilie Paterson	457
19.	Maxine Daniels	439
20.	Shani Wallis	418
21.	Marion Keene	388
22.	Jill Day	388
23.	Annie Ross	332
24.	Jean Campbell	263
25.	Annette Klooger	233

Above you see Alma Cogan—voted
Outstanding British Feminine Singer
—pointing out something of interest
to David Whitfield, runner-up in the
Outstanding British Male Singer

Topping the NME *poll for the first time, 1956.*

showmen. Even though they had come from completely different backgrounds, they had much in common. Both were true gentlemen, impeccable in dress and manners, Robert soft spoken, Bernie more outgoing. They also had in common a great admiration for Alma.

Of course, wherever Alma went there were always followers, sending flowers, notes, protestations of undying love. Alma had a knack of turning suitors into loyal friends. With most it worked. It proved more difficult, however, with one admirer – Prince Aly Khan.

Aly Khan was known for the enthusiasm with which he pursued those he admired, and Alma was given the full treatment. He sent roses to the Palladium every night for three weeks, until she finally agreed to see him. He took Alma out to a restaurant, brought her home and accepted without hesitation her polite invitation to come up for coffee. Once in the lounge, to Alma's amazement, the Prince prostrated himself at her feet, precariously balanced on one of our long, low footstools, murmuring sweet nothings in his native tongue. At this moment, Mum swept into the room. For Alma, this was hardly a surprise, as Mum always did this whenever we were alone with a man. For poor Aly Khan, however, quite unaware that she shared the flat with her family, Mum's sudden appearance must have been a terrible shock. He fell off the stool.

'Mother,' said Alma, 'I'd like you to meet Prince Aly Khan.'

'Of course,' said my mother, not in the least disconcerted to find a prince on his hands and knees on the carpet in the middle of the night. 'You own racehorses, don't you? Have you got a good tip for Ascot?'

He never reappeared.

While in *Rockin' the Town*, Alma began a twenty-six week series of her own on Radio Luxembourg, as well as a number of TV shows. These were televised in the evening. To fit them in, Alma had to finish the first Palladium show, leap into Stan's car, race to the TV studio, do her numbers and then race back to the Palladium for the second show. The police, grateful for all the charity dates she had done for them, made sure that every light was green as they sped up Oxford Street.

That year Alma did Britain's first rock and roll commercial, a thirty-second jingle on Radio Luxembourg: 'You wash it in the morning. You wash it at night. Whatever time you wash it, your hair shines bright.' She always said the hardest thing about that job was trying to stop laughing long enough to finish singing.

It certainly did Alma no harm. In November for the first time she topped the *NME* poll, ahead of Lita Roza, Anne Shelton and Ruby Murray. She was also, for the third time, top of the *Daily Mirror* poll. When Tommy Trinder presented her with the *Daily*

Back in Brighton as a star.

1956: a musicians' strike at the BBC threatens to disrupt the first episode of Alma's new TV series. Alma is reduced to rehearsing at home to the accompaniment of her tape recorder.

Mirror statuette on a special Sunday night TV programme at the Palladium, she said, with tears running down her cheeks, 'Oh dear, I've probably rusted it! I can't believe how lucky I am!'

She was now indisputedly Britain's most popular girl singer, and was invited to the USA to appear on *The Ed Sullivan Show*. She had in fact already been invited earlier in the year, but had had to decline because of her Palladium commitments.

At that time most stars would have sacrificed everything for an invitation to appear on *The Ed Sullivan Show*. It was the biggest TV show of its day, watched by millions. Only the most successful US stars were ever asked, and scarcely any singers from outside the USA. Yet now for the second time Alma had to turn him down. As a winner in the *NME* poll she felt she must appear at the big annual concert the paper put on in February for its readers. Perhaps Ed Sullivan was fascinated by someone who apparently treated his invitation so lightly. Alma was invited to 'take a rain check on it, and come in April.'

So she sang her new song, 'You, Me and Us', at the Albert Hall in February and then in New York in April. It was her first visit to the States, and it was a triumph.

Lew Grade recalls: 'Alma was a very dear and extremely talented lady – one of our favourite artistes. When she got a call from *The Ed Sullivan Show* in America, I got in touch with Ed, who was a very good friend, and asked if she could do two songs instead of the usual one, which he invariably had his guest singers do. . . . He agreed, and she was a smash. It was a very big deal in those days for a new British singer to be such an immediate hit on what was the most prestigious variety show in America.'

'Tell London that you knocked 'em dead,' Ed Sullivan scrawled across the running order programme sheet after her debut on his show. With Alma on the programme sheet that evening were ten of the biggest names in American show business, including Judy Holliday, Sydney Chaplin, Paul Douglas, Kay Thompson and Henry Fonda. It was a souvenir well worth bringing home, especially as it was accompanied by an invitation to return.

Alma could always be relied upon to do whatever she could for charity. Here she sings for 450 disabled ex-servicemen at a Buckingham Palace garden party.

More immediately she had another series to do for BBC TV. Her guests on the first two programmes were two of her favourite comedians, Dick Bentley and Harry Secombe.

As usual, Lily Anthony made some breathtaking gowns to Alma's designs. One of these, a frothy, pale pink creation strewn with feathers, was only completed just before the performance and there was no time for a full dress rehearsal. Alma swept through an archway at the opening and the dress caught on a jutting nail. With the cameras full on her, she lightly tried to tug it free, but the only response was an unnerving rending of material. As the skirt had been torn almost in two, she simply chuckled, threw the trailing material over her shoulder and went right on with the song.

The audience loved it. The BBC, however, was horrified – not so much that they might be made a laughing stock, but that Alma might sue them. Much to their relief, that never occurred to her. She just thought it funny.

On one of her tours, she was appearing with The Goons – Harry Secombe, Michael Bentine, Peter Sellers and Spike Milligan. She had just finished her big ballad with her arms outstretched in front of her, when one of them ran on stage and put a huge lump of ice in her hands. When Alma phoned home that night, she told us about it: 'There I was, standing on stage with this ice dripping down my frock. You had to laugh . . . the audience certainly did, and of course, there were guffaws from the wings.'

Humour was becoming more and more a feature of her act anyway. *Picture Post* had summed up the three leading British girl singers very neatly: 'Roza uses sex, Regan sentiment. Cogan prefers humour to put her point across, and she uses it well.'

Once she had use it to save her face in what could have been the most embarrassing incident in her career. It was at another of the staff parties at Windsor Castle. Still unaccustomed to such an audience, Alma was unusually nervous. The band struck up for the opening song of her act and out she came, sang the first few bars of 'From This Moment On', slipped and fell

flat on her face at the feet of the Queen Mum. As she picked herself up, she winked and said, 'Nobody sleeps while I'm on.' The Royal Family loved it and she was asked back again and again.

Alma's musical director, Stan, was once a victim of her humour. He had a new dinner suit made of mohair. The first time he wore it, he felt especially elegant as he began the show as he always did, advancing through the curtain with the traditional cry, 'Ladies and Gentlemen, Miss Alma Cogan.' The curtain was now supposed to be drawn gently back, giving Stan time to walk calmly to the piano and strike the opening bars for Alma's entrance. On this occasion, however, the stage hand drew the curtain back at such a pace that Stan had to sprint to the piano in time to be seated and start the music. As he did so, there was an ominous sound of ripping cloth. One leg of the new trousers had split from thigh to heel.

Waiting to rehearse for her second appearance in a Royal Command Performance, Alma sits in the 'audience' with Winifred Atwell. Winnie and her husband and manager, Lou, became great mates and frequent visitors to the flat.

Stan played doggedly on. After all, there was no immediate problem. He was seated behind the piano and the audience could not see his legs. Trouble began only when Alma came across, as she always did after the first song, to introduce him to the audience. To her amazement he stayed sitting. 'Stand up!' she hissed, then repeated the introduction. Still no move from Stan. 'I can't get up,' he hissed back. 'Look at my trousers.'

Alma started giggling, then turned and broadcast his predicament to the audience. There was nothing for Stan to do but brazen it out. Disregarding the flapping trouser and bare leg, he got to his feet, moved forward and bowed. The audience,

Sunday Night at the London Palladium. Left to right: *David Whitfield, Eddie Calvert, Dickie Valentine, Alma, Ted Heath, Winifred Atwell, Anne Shelton, Tommy Trinder.*

Opposite: *Bob Monkhouse, Vera Lynn, Count Basie, Margot Fonteyn and Max Bygraves are among those being presented to the Queen at a Royal Command Performance.*

Below: *There was an extraordinary bill for that show: Alma appeared with her favourite ladies of song, Vera Lynn and Gracie Fields.*

convinced that it was all part of the act, loved it and by the end of the show, Alma and he had turned the trousers into such a feature that Stan was worried that Alma would want him in torn trousers for the rest of the run.

About this time, the musical content of Alma's act began to change, especially when she was doing TV shows. She still included her own latest hits, but as the programmes grew in length she had the chance to include many of the swinging songs that she enjoyed, but did not record. This was becoming a source of some tension between her and Wally. Wally, having found the songs that made her name, wanted her to maintain that style on all her records. She wanted to broaden her range.

Alma was back in London in June 1956, appearing at the Hippodrome for four weeks with Lonnie Donegan, whose skiffle music was almost as popular as rock and roll. For the

first time she was back in the theatre where her London career had begun – in the chorus of *High Button Shoes*. Nostalgically she revisited the dressing room she had shared with Audrey Hepburn, stared in the same mirror and wondered at how far they had both come since then.

After the Hippodrome, she and Stan were off again round the country and making plans for a second visit to America at the end of the year. Then disaster struck.

Alma told me about it in a letter: 'Dear Sandra. A terrible thing . . . When I got home last Saturday there was a message

Alma in her Palladium dressing room with her musical director, pianist and friend of many years, Stan Foster.

from Stan's mum. When I phoned she told me Stan had been in a terrible accident. They wouldn't let me in to see him until 8 a.m. . . . . naturally I didn't get any sleep. When I saw him it was awful . . . covered in bandages . . . his legs were in splints . . . all broken bones . . . lucky to be alive. He was just barely conscious and all he was worried about was his hands . . . they seemed to be OK. . . . His folks were in a terrible state, as you can imagine. I talked to them for a little while and tried to make them feel better. The doctors aren't saying much . . . they don't know how long he'll have to stay in hospital. I'll keep you posted.'

It took over a year for Stan to recover completely. During that time Alma visited him as often as she could, doing her best to keep his spirits up. She had to keep her own up, too. It was a stressful year for her. She greatly missed Stan's support, not only on stage but off as well. Her career was going extremely well and the demands on her time were greater than ever.

She found consolation, as she so often did in times of stress, in religion and prayer. It will come as a surprise to many people, even close friends, to know that Alma was deeply religious. On all her travels, whether local or international, she carried what she called her lucky Bible with her. I never saw her more distraught than the time she had stopped in front of the flat, set her bag down to pay the cab, turned and found the bag had disappeared. She came upstairs in a state of total despair, feeling the loss of several pieces of valuable jewellery much less than the loss of the Bible that had been a gift from Dad.

Most of her prayers during this time were, of course, for Stan's recovery.

8

'We're Just Good Friends

THE MOST important engagement that Stan missed in 1957 was one that resulted from the success of Alma's appearance on *The Ed Sullivan Show* in the spring: an invitation to star in December at the Persian Room at the Plaza Hotel in New York. Alma was, naturally, a bit apprehensive, the more so since the Persian Room's regular star was the great Lena Horne.

In November, just before she set out for New York, Alma was asked to be one of a group of British stars to appear with Judy Garland on the opening night of Judy's engagement at the Dominion Theatre. It was in this show that the American comedian Alan King made his British début. He and Alma became friends later on. Alma, of course, watched Judy closely, to learn from her as much as she could. She even took the opportunity to ask Judy for some specific advice on how to prepare for the Persian Room.

Judy suggested that Alma get hold of Dick Masters, who had staged her own act. Alma did, and his advice was invaluable and reassuring.

She took a dozen dresses with her to the Plaza, and the suitcases were endless. For the act she decided to be even more British than she was at home, and included 'I'm Queen of the Cockneys', a song that she had come across just before she left England.

On the first night, when she looked through the curtains and saw Cecil B. De Mille sitting there alongside Ginger Rogers, she nearly fled. Here in front of her were some of the greats of our movie-going youth. Would they even stop eating to listen

Family reunion at the Plaza, New York – Mum, Alma, me and Ivor.

to her? They did, and they loved her, especially the Cockney number. She was a hit.

It so happened that I was in the USA at that time myself. A girlfriend of mine, Felice Gordon, and I had decided to make it big on Broadway, but after weeks of pounding the pavements we ended up in Miami Beach, Florida. She had got a job at the reception desk at the Fontainbleau Hotel, and I had been a cocktail waitress for two nights when I heard that Alma and Mum were ensconced for six weeks in the most expensive hotel in New York. I took a train and joined them for Christmas. Ivor arrived from Denver and we had a family reunion.

Life at the Plaza was certainly stylish. They had given Alma a huge suite. It was not until the end of the engagement that Alma discovered that though the suite was free, room service was not. She and Mum had been ordering meal after meal for friends – and, as it was Christmas, a turkey lunch for all of us. When it was time to leave, her fee for the cabaret only just covered the bill.

Alma arrived home just in time to appear at the *NME* concert, where for the second year she received the trophy for the most popular female British singer – 'A great honour that I would not miss even for the chance of another US tour,' she said.

In 1958 she made six new records, and her first album *I Love to Sing*. The album was received very well, but it was a surprise. Instead of her usual novelty songs she had recorded a mixture of standards and even a jazz version of 'Blue Skies', which many of her fans had never heard before. It would have been less of a surprise in America, as Alma had added a number of jazz songs to her repertoire at the Plaza, and had been hailed as 'Britain's best jazz singer'.

Pleased with her New York triumph, Alma was at the Manchester Hippodrome that spring, and at Morecambe with Semprini in the summer. She also had her own nine-week series on BBC radio, a half-hour slot on Sundays entitled *Sunday Best*, as well as guest appearances on a variety of popular TV programmes, most frequently *The Billy Cotton Band Show*. She was

Alma with Judy Garland, her husband Sid Luft, and comedian Alan King.

Billy's favourite guest and she appeared on the show eleven times in all, very largely because she and Billy always enjoyed themselves – and their enjoyment was infectious. Billy, like his son, Bill Junior, who was now a producer at the BBC, soon became a close friend of the family, and he and Mum would spend hours reminiscing about the pre-war shows they had enjoyed in their youth.

Jimmy Henney, Alma's long-time friend from Chappells Music, recalls: 'We called ourselves "The Rat Pack" . . . Alma, Shirley (Burt, as we used to call her) Bassey, Joan Regan, Ronnie Carroll and me. We would go everywhere together and if Alma, Shirley or Joan didn't have a date for a première or an opening night, I would do the honours. As my lovely wife, Ginetta, preferred to stay at home on those occasions, I was the perfect escort.'

That summer I was working in London, doing a Bryan Blackburn revue at the Stork Club which was, at that time, *the* place to be. It was an 'intimate' club, which is a euphemism for small and crowded. The stage was the size of a postage stamp, and during my first week there, I fell off it. At the time American stars who were in London to make a film would come to the Stork Club, so when I made my entrance and saw Richard Widmark sitting just a yard or two away I was thrown – literally – off balance and nearly fell into his lap. It got a big laugh and I covered my embarrassment by pretending it was part of the show.

Alma and Jimmy Henney, the self-styled 'perfect escort', one of 'The Rat Pack'.

Throughout 1959, with Stan now back on stage with her, Alma worked even more intensively, although they did not move around so hectically now. Generally they did six-week seasons, put together by the Grade Agency, then moved on, often with the same stars on the bill. One of the best bills was at Manchester: Alma, Eric Morecambe, Ernie Wise, Billy Dainty, Freddy Frinton and the Dallas Boys. Most of them stayed at a country club nearby.

For Eric in particular the country club was a haven from his fans. At least Alma's fans did not demand a song in the middle

Alma with Benny Hill on his BBC show, 1958. He loved working with her: 'We had great fun. We did six TV shows together and in all that time, under all that pressure, I never once saw her get cross or angry.'

of the street, but poor Eric was forever being pestered by people who expected him to make them laugh there and then. She and Eric became firm friends at this time – and right at the end of her life he was one of the few people she particularly asked to see.

Alma had a passion for second-hand records and one day in the Charing Cross Road she had noticed a battered old disc without even a label. Just out of curiosity, she bought it for a shilling. When she played it that evening, Mum recognized it immediately. 'That's "Last Night on the Back Porch",' she said. 'It was very popular when I was young.' She went to the piano and played entirely from memory. Alma liked it, recorded it and

A charity lunch with Petula Clark (left), *Johnnie Ray (holding the* hors d'oeuvre) *and Anne Shelton* (right).

introduced it on TV one night, accompanied by the whole of the studio audience, whom she had taught to sing it with her during the warm-up session.

When I had a two-week break from the Stork Club, Alma suggested we go to Italy. We booked into the Excelsior on the Lido in Venice. It was an enormous, magnificent hotel in the oldest traditional style. We loved it. Alma relaxed and we both fell in love with the songs that were played constantly on the radio and wherever we went – 'Amore' and 'Come Prima', sung by Moreno Marini. We also found out that it is true what they say about Italian men: they do pinch your bottoms – anyway, they did in the late 1950s. Alma recorded 'Amore' on our return home.

Behind the desk at the hotel was an absolutely gorgeous, very tall, blond young man. His name was Sergio Novak. While we were having lunch, Alma said, 'Sergio's definitely for Shirley Bassey. I must fix it.' When we got home, she phoned Shirley and said, 'You just have to drop everything and go to the Excelsior Hotel in Venice and check out the chap on the desk.' Within a year Shirley and Sergio were married!

When we were both on tour at the same time, Alma and I would keep in touch and arrange to meet in some town halfway between us. On one occasion I was in Bradford, touring with Sandy Wilson's musical *The Boyfriend*, while Alma was doing a Sunday concert at the Leeds Empire. I was able to take some friends, Colin Hopkins and two mates from the show, Larry Drew and Graham James, to see Alma perform. Afterwards, we all went to dinner. My friends were thrilled. Sometimes I would forget the effect Alma had on people. I was just visiting my sister. They were meeting a star.

Later Colin became a very successful agent with William Morris. While I was in America, Alma approached Colin and said, 'Why don't you come and work for me? We know all the same people and it would be a big help.'

'I was getting a bit bored with my job,' Colin says, 'and being part of Alma's world sounded like it might be fun – and it was. When I wasn't busy organizing things for Alma, Fay

A portrait by Vivienne, one of the great photographers of her day.

would find things for me to do – like helping to rearrange the furniture at one o'clock in the morning. I did put in strange hours. I remember one time I was leaving the flat at about 10.30 p.m., and Fay said, "Half day, Colin?"

'Sometimes she would say, "I'm going out to post a letter." I would say, "Fay, it's midnight." We all knew she was going to the casino.' Mum posted a lot of midnight letters.

It was in 1959 that Alma for once hit the headlines rather more often than she wished. It all because of Cary Grant, who was in London that year to make a film called *The Grass is Greener*.

As children, Alma and I had read movie magazines the way other children read comics. We knew the names and films of every star and for us those stars were idols. Imagine how thrilled I was when Alma came home one night to tell us that she had spent the evening staring across Jack Isow's restaurant straight into the eyes of the man we had always felt to be the most glamorous of all – Cary Grant. She said she had managed to be very cool about it and had tried to concentrate her attention on her companions and her food.

The following day she went to a different restaurant. So did Cary Grant. Again they had chosen the same one. Again she stared. He stared back. They did not meet.

The third evening, at yet another restaurant, there he was again. This time he came right over to the table. He explained that he had discovered who she was, but assured her that the choice of restaurants was a complete coincidence. However, he thought they should build on it. Would she come out with him next evening? Deciding that it was the work of Fate, Alma agreed.

At first there were no problems, no publicity, but then they went to a première together and, inevitably, were photographed. Alma tried to keep the press off their trail by keeping him from the flat. Mum and I rebelled. A compromise was reached. Alma would bring him home only if we made a game of it. I must act as the maid and Mum as the cook.

That evening we were waiting, fully prepared to play our rôles in this charade, only for them to be late – very late.

'I am not waiting any more,' I said, and off I went and had a bath. Twenty minutes later out I came into the hall swathed in an old dressing gown, with my hair hanging down over my face. I was not alone in the hall. Through my dripping hair I could see an immaculate pair of black shoes, a beautifully cut suit, and above that the face I had worshipped through a thousand romantic reels. Mumbling incoherently, I fled.

I never did discover quite how Alma explained away this

One of my favourite pictures of Alma and Mum.

*Alma being taught to play the
ukulele by Mum, who often used
to entertain us at parties, where
she was always a great attraction.*

extraordinary figure, but she did own up to the joke we had tried to play, and the next time we met at one of our parties Cary was too tactful to refer to any earlier visit to the flat.

'Cary's got a fine sense of humour and I like him,' Alma assured the *Daily Express* in one of a series of responses on the subject. 'That's all there is to it. We're just good friends.'

It was true. They were very good friends and they made no secret of it. One press photographer hid under Cary's car to get a picture that would be featured right across the front page with Alma's quote: 'Please, no photographs. It is so embarrassing.' On the other hand, the paper could hardly accuse them of trying to go unnoticed. The car number was CG 1.

Four stars of the day with their mothers – Marty Wilde, Alma, Tommy Bruce and Cliff Richard.

'CG', as Alma used to call him, loved sausages and mash. He used to say, 'I was raised on the stuff, and it's still a treat.' I'd love to have seen the faces of the regulars in some local pub when Alma Cogan and Cary Grant casually strolled in and ordered platters of this down-to-earth fare. 'CG' accepted with good humour Alma's teasing him for his well-earned repuation for thrift. Every time he opened his wallet, she would say, 'Look out, here come the moths.'

Benny Hill recalls that in 1960 he was in a show at the Palace called *Fine Fettle*. 'I heard that Alma was out front with Cary Grant. When we had a chance to chat later, she told me that they had gone to a coffee stall and Cary had made a fuss because he felt he had been short-changed by twopence. When he was pursuing her, instead of the usual flowers and chocolate, he would bring her the cotton sewing sachets from his hotel room, saying, "Well, we don't want to waste them, do we?"'

Over the next six months, while Cary was making the film,

Alma's love of dress design never left her and she spent a lot of time designing dresses for her act.

Just two of Alma's many album covers.

he and Alma saw a lot of each other. For her birthday party, she took over an entire Italian restaurant, the Versailles, and invited forty guests. Cary acted as host and part-time waiter too. He even acted as bouncer, throwing out some gate-crashers. Sadly I was away on tour and missed that historic occasion.

There was also a report in the press that got back to Hollywood. The columnist Sheilah Graham reported that they held hands and that Cary Grant 'generally looked like a man in love.' One of his biographers quoted him as saying that Alma Cogan was 'the sweetest girl in the world. She has brains, talent, a sense of humour and a wonderful sense of understanding.' The writer concluded, 'Cary has neglected to mention whether his third wife, Betsy, thinks Alma is wonderful too.'

Whatever she thought, when *The Grass is Greener* opened in London a year later, Betsy came too. Since he had finished the film, CG had kept in touch with Alma by letter and by phone. He sent her tickets for the première. Alma and he continued to assure the press that they were just good friends, but after Betsy's arrival, Alma thought it better to keep out of the picture. She once told Jackie Collins, 'The world is full of married men'; Jackie later used this as the title of her first novel.

People still ask me how intimate Alma and CG really were, and I can't tell them. It seems strange now, but, close as we were during all our growing-up years and even though we talked about everything and anything there was to talk about, the one thing we never discussed or divulged were details of our sex lives. Maybe it was the difference in our ages or maybe it was simply the way we were raised. But I did discover how much he cared for her.

Many years later, soon after Alma's death, I was dining with a friend, Robert Rayne, in a very smart New York restaurant when I saw Cary Grant across the room. I wrote a note. At first the waiter would not take it, assuming that we were simply young fans trying to get an autograph. Eventually I persuaded him. Cary read the note, looked up, saw me and ran across the restaurant. Then he sat down and talked and talked about Alma, and as he talked, he cried.

9

Around the World in Eighty Dresses

*P*ERHAPS MY most vivid memory of Alma is of her standing in the middle of her bedroom, with the room filled with dresses that she was somehow going to fit into what appeared to be totally inadequate suitcases. Throughout her career Alma travelled further and more frequently than any other British singer of her day. As soon as one of her records started selling well in any country overseas, she would try to make time for a visit.

Alma's first overseas tour was in 1958, to one of the smallest markets of all. She went to Iceland, where she had had a big success with 'Never Do a Tango with an Eskimo', even though Eskimos were as foreign to Iceland as they were to Britain. Until then, no British singer had been to Iceland – unless perhaps aboard Viking longships. Alma did ten concerts in ten days.

That meant ten long-distance telephone calls as well. Alma always rang home every night, wherever she was, to assure Mum that all was fine. To telephone from Blackpool was no major operation, but from Reykjavik it could be traumatic. The phones were extremely erratic.

'I am singing in Icelandic,' she announced.

'You're joking,' said Mum. 'You don't know Icelandic.'

'I am being taught it,' Alma replied. 'It's wonderful here. Why don't you come and listen to me?'

'Well, dear, what a nice idea. Maybe next time.'

Mum in Iceland? She complained of the cold in Kensington in June. Alma was left to keep in touch by phone.

Alma's suggestion of having Mum in Iceland was hardly

Alma and Rosemary Squires with two of Alma's mates and co-performers, Eric Morecambe and Ernie Wise, at the Manchester Palace, 1961.

serious, but her decision to sing in Icelandic most certainly was. It was not that she had learned the language – at least no more than to manage a friendly 'good morning' – but she had learned how to mimic it. She had then mastered the words of an Icelandic song and sang it in Icelandic. It was a great success and it was a ploy that she was to use to increasing effect throughout her trips abroad.

Alma was an excellent mimic. She and I were always doing accents and dialects. I suppose it was thanks to our movie upbringing, watching all those wonderful character actors. She regularly included take-offs of other singers in her act. Once Alma, Joan Regan, Shirley Bassey and Vera Lynn were all at a party given by Maurice Kinn, the owner of *NME*, and his wife Berenice. As a party piece Alma did perfect imitations of the other three.

Her first Irish trip was also in 1958. From the coverage in the English press you might have thought she had gone just to kiss the Blarney Stone, though few people had less need of its magical properties. She was really there to do sixteen dance-hall concerts.

The Irish dance halls were surprisingly well appointed, except for the pianos. They were nearly always upright, often antique. Stan was faced with one piano on which some of the notes stayed down when struck – most of the time. After that, he included in their contract a requirement that every venue had to have a grand piano.

Everything went beautifully, until they came to a dance hall where there was nothing but another of those big upright pianos. Stan did not even bother to go near it. He went straight up to the manager and simply presented the contract.

'Here is the contract,' said Stan. 'Where is the grand piano?'

'Sure, it's there,' replied the manager. 'Isn't this the grandest piano you ever did see in your life?'

It wasn't, and for Stan the concert was absolute purgatory. For Alma it was simply a joke. So it was for Eric Morecambe and Ernie Wise when they heard of it, for it was out of that story that they created their famous – and very funny – TV

With Derek Goodman, one of the millionaires who fell in love with her during her visit to South Africa.

Britain's 'Ambassadress of Song': laden with souvenirs on her return from South Africa.

sketch about 'the grandest piano you ever did see in your life'.

'Alma is fast becoming Britain's Ambassadress of Song,' wrote *NME* when she went on her third trip, this time to South Africa. She was very well known there through *Take It From Here*. Radio was particularly important in South Africa because at that time there was no television. But it was her appearance in person that made the major impact. She was booked into the Colony, the main night club in Johannesburg, run by Stanley and Bea Tolman. At home an engagement at a night club would concern only those few who could afford the price of a night out. In South Africa it was a major media event.

Among those who came to the club were two millionaires. They did not come at the same time, but they did come to the same conclusion. Both decided that they wanted to marry Alma, and both set about wooing her in their very different ways.

It was at least partly Alma's fault. In her act she included 'I Can't Give You Anything But Love'. With this song, to add to the effect, she always picked out a man in the audience to sing it to. One night this had considerably more effect than she had bargained for. Two dozen roses were immediately delivered to her dressing room, followed by an invitation to dinner. Quite unintentionally Alma had been serenading Derek Goodman, the international polo player.

Derek had once been Zsa Zsa Gabor's boyfriend and was now determined to be Alma's. He lived in a house that Alma told us 'looked like a castle surrounded by Martinis'. He pursued her with roses from Johannesburg to her next engagement in Durban, then telephoned Mum to enlist her support in persuading Alma to stay on in South Africa. This was a tactical mistake. Mum had nothing against millionaires, but was certainly not going to help one keep her Alma overseas.

The other millionaire, Bernie Lazarus, was a young motor-business tycoon. Rather shy and retiring, his was very much the approach of the serious suitor. He offered a diamond ring and, when that was rejected, persuaded Alma at least to keep his watch.

When she returned to England, it was to find that both Derek and Bernie were in pursuit. Alma, however, made it clear she had no intention of marrying either of them. In the end they both came to accept this, though we saw a lot of them at the flat meanwhile.

For the next few years, Alma's travels took her to Israel several times and on a number of trips round Europe, mostly to France and Germany. Then in 1961 she decided to go even further and she spent only three of the next twelve months in Britain. First she set off on a trip that would take her to Kenya and Spain. In Kenya her trick of singing in the native language came badly unstuck. On foreign tours Alma always came back to start the second part of her programme with 'Mack the

Opposite: *In Berlin, dressed as a Pearly Queen.*

Below: *Alma was a great hit on a visit to a school in Israel. At the time, she had a number one record called 'Fly Me to the Moon'.*

Knife'. She used to get someone to translate into the local language a few sentences that she would then insert into the song – something like 'It is nice to be here'. She would learn the words phonetically, as she had done on that first visit to Iceland. She was quick at learning words, and it used to go down very well.

In Kenya she and Stan asked the drummer, who had been acting as their interpreter, to translate her messages into Swahili. 'No trouble,' he said. But this time when she started singing the words, instead of the usual ripple of appreciative

With a worried looking kangaroo in Australia, and a friendly lion cub in Kenya.

applause from the audience there was first of all an ominous silence, then a ripple of laughter – and there should not have been laughter. What was more puzzling was that it was clearly embarrassed laughter. At the end of the song Alma got tremendous applause, but she and Stan both knew something had gone wrong. It was not until the end of the concert that the owners of the hotel told her what it was. Thanks to the drummer, she had cheerfully been singing a string of Swahili obscenities. She never knew what they were, as no one could face translating them back to her.

Presumably she was forgiven, as she was asked out to lunch in Nairobi by the Countess of Kenmare. To Alma, that seemed reassuringly conventional. No one was going to play tricks on her in a Countess's house. Lunch was delicious, everyone was very complimentary about the concert and Alma was taken out to admire the garden. There the Countess called for Tana. 'Her dog?' thought Alma. No. Out from behind a bush strode a full-grown lion.

Alma shrieked, threw her handbag in the air and ran up the garden into the house. The lion was left playing with her make-up and money. 'Tana was much more frightened by your shriek than you were of her,' the Countess assured her guest. Alma was not so sure.

That year Alma established another record. She became the only British artiste to record a pop song in six different languages. It was called variously 'Dis-lui', or 'Sage ihm', or 'Dígale', or 'Dirgli' or 'Itte kudesai' or simply 'Tell Him', depending on whether you were French, German, Spanish, Italian, Japanese or English.

In June 1962, Alma was off to Japan for six weeks. By chance her record 'He Just Couldn't Resist Her with Her Pocket Transistor' had been released in Japan the previous year – to dramatic effect. In Japanese eyes, Alma's record was a celebration of Japanese technology. They loved it. It topped the charts for an unprecedented ten months, twice fighting off a challenge from Elvis Presley and selling hundreds of thousands of copies.

The Japanese record market at that time was second in size only to that of the United States. (Germany came third, ahead of France and Britain.) When Alma arrived there were at least fifty photographers and newsreel presenters there to meet her. Questions were fired at her through interpreters, as if she were a visiting statesman. In a way she was. Pop music there was a major subject for news and comment, and to the Japanese she was an international star. It was heady stuff. There she was, thousands of miles from home, being treated like a female Elvis Presley. She found that she even had a Japanese fan club. They greeted her with presents. So did Toshiba, who had

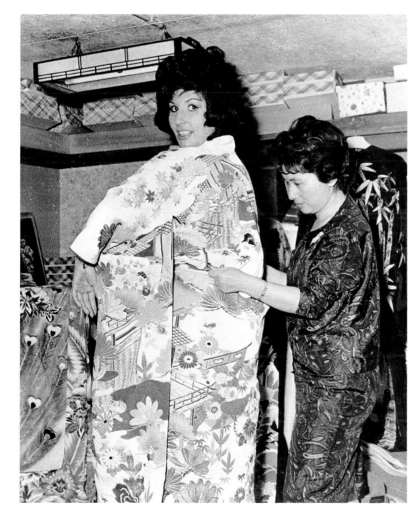

Not all Alma's clothes were her own design. She discovered kimonos on tour in Japan and bought lots of them.

'Pocket Transistor' was a massive hit in Japan and Japanese television audiences loved her.

released the record. They gave her – well, of course – a pocket transistor.

Her first concerts were in a vast night club which employed 400 hostesses. The opening night was attended by 6,000 screaming teenagers. This time she went further than before in her use of the local tongue – not easy in a language in which she found that even her own name had changed: she was known as 'Aruma'. She introduced her programme herself and sang the latest local hit – both of them in Japanese. The audience was so delighted that they clapped throughout the song. Alma was not certain if she was hurt or relieved that they could not possibly have heard her efforts at the words.

It was in Tokyo that Alma did her first colour TV show. 'The effect of the dresses in colour was out of this world,' she said. 'It gave me more scope for my bigger and better gowns.' She was well equipped for the challenge, having taken a revolutionary step to solve her usual luggage problem. Each of her dresses usually had up to 300 yards of material in the skirt, but for this trip she had put 300 yards into one petticoat, which would go under all her dresses. This meant, of course, that the dresses themselves were much smaller, and left her room in the luggage for all the outfits she needed for the tour.

Of course, she spent lots of time in the shops, buying kimonos galore. She came back with a stock of them, including some for Mum and me, and dolls in glass cases that she had been given as presents. The Japanese women loved Alma in all her gear, especially as she made special efforts to speak to them and sign her autograph in Japanese. In the hotels, too, she took her shoes off and sat on the floor, as that was the custom. It was also tactful. At five foot seven she towered over both men and women, so when she stood up she felt like a giant.

One of her concerts was in the open air, in a football stadium. Somehow they had rigged up curtains. Stan made his usual opening announcement, which he had learnt to do in Japanese: 'Ladies and Gentlemen, Alma Cogan.' The curtains opened. By this time Stan was at the piano, with his back to the audience. He saw Alma step forward, then freeze, just for a moment,

before she started to sing. He turned round and saw why. There were 38,000 people in the stadium.

On some of Alma's tours, especially those that took her around Australia (which she visited next in 1962, for the first of three successive years), the Grade Agency would send out a manager to look after the travelling arrangements. Alma would appear either at the Chequers night club, on TV or in concert, perhaps doing a whole *Alma Cogan Show* or appearing as the guest on an Australian show with its own Australian stars.

When she went as far as Australia, Alma would usually add on a few weeks in Hong Kong, Singapore or Honolulu, and then return by way of the USA. Ten days in the USA would give her and Stan a break from performance and a chance to see friends such as Sammy Davis Jr.

Sammy was one of Alma's closest friends. He had first come to London in 1960. They met after his fabulous opening night at the Pigalle. It was packed, and a queue of British stars – Tony Newley, Yvie and Leslie Bricusse and Lionel Blair – trooped round to Sammy's dressing room after the show to tell him he was the greatest. On and on it went, till Alma swept in. 'That,' she said in her most disdainful tone, 'was just about the worst performance I have ever seen.' There was an appalled silence, then Sammy collapsed with shouts of laughter.

It was the beginning of a very special friendship for both of them. It was not just because they shared the same taste for the ludicrous and refused to take themselves too seriously; it went deeper. 'It was,' said Sammy, 'almost as if someone had said, "I know he does not have many friends in London, so I shall offer my hand in friendship." She was always there when she was needed.'

On one of her visits to the USA, Alma found Sammy filming in Hollywood by day and doing cabaret in Las Vegas by night. One day Sammy took her with him to Hollywood, where Judy Garland hosted a dinner in her honour, and she spent a day on the set of *Robin and the Seven Hoods*. Everyone is supposed to remember where they were on the day JFK was shot. I remember

At Heathrow on her return from Madrid she was reduced to borrowing one of the stewards' jackets to protect her from the rain.

Alma telephoning us in great distress, describing how at one moment she had been laughing at the seemingly endless wise-cracking between Frank Sinatra and Dean Martin, and the next crouching with them round a transistor at the poolside listening to the unbelievable news from Dallas.

Another time, when Alma and Stan arrived unannounced in Las Vegas, they felt very much the same as Sammy had done in London. Stan hailed a cab and said, 'The best hotel.'

'Everything is taken, buddy,' said the cabby. 'It has got to be

On one trip down from Glasgow she left her luggage on the train and had to borrow shoes from Anne Shelton.

Off to Sweden in a sari she had acquired on her travels.

On holiday in Venice having a laugh with Lionel Blair.

on the other side of the strip, the bad side.'

The hotel they were taken to was in fact superb, but it was not the Sands. The Sands was where Jerry Lewis was doing his last night of cabaret. Alma had met Jerry when he first appeared with Dean Martin at the Palladium many years before. She managed to arrange for me to meet him backstage after we saw the show, only for me to break down in floods of tears at the excitement of shaking hands with my hero. He was very kind to a nervous twelve-year-old and found me a Kleenex. I carefully preserved it pressed in a book, not dreaming that years later I would be starring with him in a movie called, most appropriately, *Don't Lower the Bridge, Raise the Water*.

Alma and Stan managed to get a table that night at the Sands and Jerry joined them after the show.

'Where are you staying?' he demanded.

'We couldn't get in here,' she said. 'There are conferences in town. We are staying on the other side of the strip.'

'You don't want to stay there,' said Jerry. He picked up the telephone. 'Give me reception,' he said. 'I want the Churchill suite for Miss Cogan . . . I don't care the hell who's in there, get him out . . . And do you want a suite, Stan . . .? No? A room, then? Fine.'

The Churchill Suite had seven rooms, and Stan's room would have been called a suite in any other hotel. However, when they went to pay the bill, they were told there was no charge: 'You are guests of Mr Lewis. If I took a penny from you I'd lose my job,' said the receptionist. Mr Lewis apparently owned sixty per cent of the hotel!

It was a fair distance from Irish dance halls to the Churchill Suite, but with Alma the difference was not all that great. In both, as all around the world, she felt she was with friends.

10

Name Dropping

$\mathcal{B}$ACK HOME for a while, Alma started on her own series of spectacular TV shows. In the first one she tap-danced (she had never done it before and rehearsing slimmed her down five pounds), sang a variety of songs and hosted the whole performance. It was a foretaste not just of the series but of the style of all the *Alma Cogan Shows* to follow. Alma loved hosting her own shows, as it gave her the chance to extend her range as an all-round performer. Whenever she could, she invited good friends such as Pearl Carr and Teddy Johnson and Russ Conway to be guest stars: she loved working with her mates.

About this time, she also did a pilot for a television comedy series called *The Secret Keepers*. She played a detective in what she described as a mickey-take of a serious crime drama. Jess Conrad, Frankie Howerd and Cardew Robinson were her co-stars. At one point in the script, Alma had to go to the window and open it to throw coins to the person singing in the street below. It was Shirley Bassey, making a guest appearance. Shirley was married to the producer, Kenneth Hume.

Alma still did variety shows as well, but only in the major towns. I especially remember that she was away in Blackpool doing a summer season when Ivor dropped a bombshell at home. One evening he came in and said to Mum, 'Sit down. I have some news. I'm married. Her name's Lolita and she's Spanish.'

Not only was he married, he had been married for *three weeks*. He had been coming back to the flat every night since, because he did not dare to tell Mum the news. Mum, of course,

Left: *The second Royal Command dress, with gloves to match.*

Above: *With Frankie Howerd in* The Secret Keepers *pilot for TV.*

was distraught. He was her only son and he had married without even consulting her.

Alma, when we told her, took it far more calmly. She felt as I did: it was fine so long as Ivor was happy. It took a while, but Mum came around. Ivor brought Lolita up to the flat to meet us and it wasn't long before she was one of the family. Within a year they had a lovely son named Mark (after Dad) and, many years later, a beautiful daughter, Yolanda.

In the early 1960s, Alma and I were especially close, as I was working mostly in London and she was doing so much on TV that she would spend several days a week in the flat. She also always made a point of bringing her friends along to any theatre where I was appearing.

I was terribly nervous whenever Alma came to my shows,

Opposite: *At the Palladium with Norman Vaughan, Alan Freeman, Vera Lynn, Bert Weedon and, in front, Pete Murray and David Jacobs.*

Below: *The 1960 Royal Variety Show at the Victoria Palace. Liberace accompanies Vera Lynn, Marion Ryan, Alma, Janette Scott, Yana and Anne Shelton.*

*The photo Terence Donovan took
for the cover of Alma's album*
How About Love.

because she was very critical. But I welcomed that, as she had
an eye for pinpointing any problems I was having. I remember
once when I had to audition for Laurence Olivier for a part in
the Chichester Festival. I was terrified. My knees were literally
knocking. As I was on my way out of the flat, Alma said,
'Don't be silly. Just think of him sitting there in his underpants.'
I did exactly that and found myself laughing in the wrong place.
I didn't get the part.

Although we were both in show business, we never felt that
we were in any way in competition with each other. It was
obvious that we were pursuing very different careers. She was a
singer, and already a major star. I was beginning to make a
name for myself as an actress and comedienne. I had also just
landed myself my first part in a West End theatre, in *And
Another Thing* at the Fortune. From there I went to the Royal
Court in *The Kitchen*, directed by John Dexter. I became good
friends with Rita Tushingham, who recalls, 'We would sit at
your home for hours trying to write a song for Alma. We did,
too – it was called "Every Time I See Your Face." We loved it.
Alma said it had possibilities – she didn't say for what!'

Sometimes, of course, our careers brought Alma and me in
touch with producers or fellow performers who were involved
in both our worlds. One such producer was Al Burnett. Al had
owned the Stork Club in the 1950s and had now opened the
Pigalle, where Alma had met Sammy Davis. The Pigalle at that
time was a fashionable restaurant with a reputation for its
cabaret, with mostly American name attractions. In addition to
Sammy Davis, Betty Hutton, Peggy Lee, Tony Bennett, Steve
Lawrence and Eydie Gorme all starred there. Then Alma was
asked to headline for two weeks.

She had material specially written for her by Lionel Bart, as
well as doing impressions of Vera Lynn, Judy Garland, Eartha
Kitt and Shirley Bassey. She also made the headlines: 'With her
choice of dress, Miss Cogan, rather than appear in one of her
"tea-cosies", has designed a dress to suit the current interest in
the 1920s. It is made entirely out of silk handkerchiefs, and
named "the dress of the 700 veils".'

It was my turn to go in support of Alma. It was a great evening. Everyone in British show business had, it seemed, decided that this was one of those major occasions no one dared miss. Alma's appearance at the Pigalle was for them a sign that British show business was no longer the poor relation of the big American system.

At this time, if Alma was not on tour or overseas – and she was abroad for a large part of every year from 1962 – there was nearly always a party at the flat on Sunday nights. Alma had always loved giving parties and as the years went by they became more frequent and more elaborate – though elaborate in a most unusual way.

Most of them had a theme. On one occasion we turned the whole flat into a junk shop, hired a tea-urn, served sausages and mash, wrote coffee-shop menus in white paint on the windows, and dressed up as Cockney flower girls. We also put price tickets on all the furniture – a joke that puzzled one American guest, who said to his wife, 'What a cute way to have a garage sale!'

Alma always called Tommy Steele 'the kid', and when he was heading for New York to star in the musical *Half a Sixpence*, we threw a children's party for him and his wife Annie. Everyone had to dress up as children. They were given a bag of sweets as they walked into the flat, and a name tag, an orange, an apple and a Coca Cola. There was no alcohol at the party, as children should not drink. For entertainment, there was a conjuror who had pigeons and rabbits, while on the floor around him in short trousers and pinnies sat some of the biggest stars of the London stage.

Tony Hawes, a writer for the BBC, would bring his equipment and show films at our parties. Usually they were classic features like *Casablanca*. This time, appropriately, he brought some Laurel and Hardy reels from his own collection. He was a Laurel and Hardy fanatic.

The next time I heard from Tony, I was living in Los Angeles. He, too, had moved there. He phoned me and said, 'Are you sitting down? I just got married.'

'Congratulations,' I said.

'To Lois Laurel,' he continued.

'That's nice,' I answered.

'Stan Laurel's daughter, you dope,' he yelled. I was thrilled for him.

In the flat there was an archway in the wall between the dining room and the lounge. Alma and I would use this as a proscenium arch to stage our 'cabaret'. One day we decided to have the wall removed to provide one large, open room. So we immediately had a party and asked the guests to sign the wall. The theme was oriental. Alma had just returned from Japan, so we had a selection of kimonos to wear. The following week when the workmen came to knock the wall down they began dropping bits of the wall out of the window into their truck below. Down went Lord and Lady Docker, Roger Moore, Vera Lynn, Mick Jagger . . . the list could go on and on. It was the ultimate in name-dropping!

For one party we decided on a country and western theme, and covered the furniture in checked gingham. When people arrived they were greeted by trays of hot dogs, crisps and pickles. Riggs O'Hara (whom I met when he came from America with the original production of *West Side Story*) was dressed and made up as a Red Indian, tending the bar. Peter O'Toole caught sight of him and called, 'Hello, son, I'd know you anywhere.' Riggs had recently played Peter's son in the film of *Becket*. Some of the other people who probably wound up with dyspepsia from too many crisps and pickles were Yvie and Leslie Bricusse, who used to call me 'Olive Oyl', and Tony Newley, who was in the first throes of his relationship with Joan Collins and had apparently forgotten to tell her about the party. Joan turned up anyway. Alan Freeman chatted to Sir Joseph Lockwood, head of EMI. Lionel Blair was teaching us the twist, which Chubby Checker had just taught him. Norma Heyman was laughing with Shelley Winters, Michael Black talking agent talk to Lila Burkeman, and Judy Garland and Albert Finney were playing boules.

Some of the parties went on all night. People came and went,

Alma loved sketching: she did these drawings of me and Lionel Bart.

One of Alma's Christmas cards – divided in half to fit on the page! – designed by our friend Michael Joseph. He took every name in Alma's address book and put them together, in no particular order, to make the candle – quite a feat. By no means all the names are well known, but one line includes 'Noël Coward, Ken Tynan, Eric Morecambe, Audrey & Leslie Grade'. Michael remembers that Christmas at Stafford Court was always special – weeks of card designing, decorations, present wrapping and exotic catering.

and a few hardy ones stayed till breakfast. Alma never tired, and was just as bright at 5 a.m. as when she began. And, of course, Mum and I would still be there as well. This was fine for me until I found myself on tour again, this time with the play *Billy Liar*. The tour would keep me away from home for a year, but I determined that, so long as I was anywhere within striking range of London, I would not miss the parties. That meant that at weekends the rest of the cast would go on to the next town, and I would take the sleeper back to London. Then I would have to get up at eight on Monday morning to make the train call at ten.

Alma was at the height of her earning power, but when Alma had money, she spent it, just like Dad. She was noted for her generosity and for the presents she used to find, or even have made specially, for her friends. Of course, as the press stories on her earnings grew, so did speculation on her love life. The millionaires were back in South Africa and Cary Grant had gone home to Hollywood; so rumours now centred on home-grown candidates, particularly on the playwright Lionel Bart.

'Alma and I had a very special relationship,' he recalls. 'She was the only one I specifically wanted to see *Oliver* during its try-out in Wimbledon, as I valued her opinion so highly. Her reaction was more than I had hoped for. "Li," she said, "this is going to be the biggest hit the West End has seen in years."'

Alma was right. We all went to the opening night. I remember counting twenty-three curtain calls, and *Oliver* ran for years. 'It seems I was always up at the flat,' Lionel says. 'Fay was an attraction there on her own. She always had a poker game going with the likes of Tommy Steele, Sean Connery and Stanley Baker, or she'd just be making sure everyone had enough to eat. One night I brought up two young actors, Terence Stamp and Michael Caine. They were appearing in my play *Why the Chicken*.'

I suppose Lionel thought there could be no better introduction to show business than a visit to the Cogan flat. I remember Mum thinking they looked undernourished. She immediately brought out a stack of sandwiches. I have to laugh when I think

Grant McKenzie, Alex Fondes, Bill Marchant, Ginetta & Jimmy Henney, Sarah & Noel Harrison Harold Miller, Joan Mullen, John Musgrove, Terry Donovan, Norman Newell, Mike Nichols, Raymond Ray, Avril & Dennis Norden, Stan, Lottie & Reuben Foster, Annie & Tommy Steele, Roy Round, Berenice, Adam, Rachel & Maurice Kinn, Melville Gilham, Jimmy Green, Sony & Bob Freeman, Peter Yarrow, Jean & Lilian Anthony, Joan & Tony Newley, Colin Clewes, Freddy Frinton, Joanna & Rex Berry, Auntie Sadie, Uncle Leslie & Ivan, Myrna Melinski, Liz & Bob Monkhouse, Stanley Mann, Peggy Mount, Mary, Cara, Tina & Peter Noble, C.G., Auntie Bee & Uncle Gerry, Alex Strickland, Mai & Sammy Davis, Bert Shevalove, Alan Tarrant, Russ Conway, Emile le Mercier, Albert Finney, Jane & Peter Asher, Stuart Hiscock, Gisella & Harvey Orkin, Truda, Ringo Starr, Robert Stigwood, Rachel & Rex Harrison, Otto Demler, Mary & Alexander Plunket-Greene, Auntie Hetty, Uncle Alf & Howard, Buddy Greco, Ethel Merman, Sir Joseph, Jerry & Walter Shenson, Pat & Larry Gelbart, Michael Mills, Gilbert Becaud, Noel Coward, Ken Tynan, Eric Morecambe, Frank Thring, Audrey & Leslie Grade, Lloyd Ravenscroft, Panda & Jimmy Allen, Johnny Speight, Donald Macleary, Ian Fawn-Mead, Marlene Dietrich, Mario, Barbara & Bernie Braden, Carole & Bernie Delfont, Judy Garland, Eric Sykes, Ray Martine, Jerry Lewis, Hermione Baddeley, Janice & Ben Gazzara, Malcolm Searle, June & Jack Neary, Sybil Burton, Leonard Sainer, Marcel Stellman, Petula & Claud Wolfe, Roddy MacDowell, Lolita, Mark & Ivor Cogan, Acela & Tony Winston, Jean & Cliff Michelmore, Shirley Bassey, Jose Luis Augustin, Peter Evans, Sergio Novak, Marje Proops, Mr & Mrs Pat Doncaster, Brian Epstein, Ronan O'Rahilly, Joe Levine, Wolf Mankowitz, Roy Price, Myra & Harry Secombe, Cyn & John Lennon, Syd Gillingham, Billy Smart, Eunice & Sidney Grace, Chris Denning, Paula & Jack Carter, Al Burnett, Alex & Geoffrey Everett, Bill, Cotton, Sylvia, Dina & Danny Kaye, Christina Foyle, Alan Freeman, Ronald Searle, Pat Aza, Ellen, Martin, Sally, Glyn Adam & Stanley Baker, Jill & Gina Gates, Ian Bevan, Don Moss, Serena Youngman, Leslie Roberts, John Schlesinger, Keith Skues, Jean Paul Agi, Gino e Giovanni Veronese, Kevin Ritchie, Francisco Bermudez, Mr Kruger, Mr Sakamaki, Blossom & Max Bygraves, Eamonn Andrews, Mike Ryan, Paul Anka, George & Alfred Black, Avril Angers, Sheila & Monty Berman, Millie & Ronnie Carroll, Nicole & Ian Bedford, Kiki Byrne, Theo Cowan, Victor Bruso, Jan Reed, Bernard Levin, Mike Frankovitch, Joe Mintz, Norma & John Heyman, Don Short, Fu Tong, Frank Sinatra, Auntie Judy & Uncle Al, Bill Ward, Donald Zec; Martin Jackson, Billy Marsh, Les Perrin, Wilfred Shackleton, Barry Aldis, Ralph & Mrs Warmington, Eric Maschwitz, Johnny Stewart, Bernie Lazarus, Yvonne & Paul Raff, W.F.Fraser, Ron Partridge, Dennis Wong, Pat Campbell, Jose Civagosqui, Alan King, Roland Slabbink, Herbie Wise, Kay Ballard, Paul McCartney, Rodger de Ramee, Sam Hughen, Arthur Muxlow, Joe Matthews, David Ellis, Diana & Dickie Dawson, Peter Coe, Nat Berlin, Bruce Forsyth, Trevor Chinn, Jim & Alice Craig, Cy & Maureen Endfield, Dan Farson, Alan Fashko, Jimmy Edwards, Mr & Mrs Lou Levy, Ernie Bogen, Dick Bentley, Donald Bruce, Pat Brand, Jimmy Watson, Mr & Mrs Michael Black, Kenneth More, Felice & Norman Bogner, Alfred & Paddy Marks, Bill Maynard, Libby & Murray Kash, Mr Imazumi, Dick Gabbe, Roy Pyke, Lila & Monty Burkeman, Jimmy Young, Lonnie Donegan, Billy Bruce, Bill Crozier, Peter Aldersley, Mr & Mrs David Jacobs, Bill Durrance, Barry O'Dee, Ronnie Waldman, Mr & Mrs Saks, Gerry Oord, Eve & Trevor Boswell, Mr & Mrs Cyril Berlin, Lionel Bart, Jess Conrad, Shaw Taylor, Jerry & Alice Dawson, Ramsden Greig, Fleur Cowles, Mr Ishizako, Adam Faith, Arthur Helliwell, Frank Ifield, Mr & Mrs Norman Luboff, Teddy Johnson & Pearl Carr, Teddy & Henk Scholten, Mr Dunton, Alec Fyne, Mr & Mrs Ted Heath, Lottie Albert, Tony Hall, Peter Brough, Babs & Teddy Beverley, Mr & Mrs Stanley Block, Allen Aynsworth, Mr & Mrs Ted Brennan, Frank Cordell, Don Wardell, C.R.Willis, John Miles, Anne Steele, Laurie Henshaw, Wally Ridley, Howard French, Keith Devon, Jack Upfold, Vivienne, Geoff Bole, Shirley Abicair, Pepper Davis, Bill Hearne, Johnny Mathis, Jack Dinken, Robert Clary, Mr & Mrs Schumer, Steve O'Hurran, Shelley Winters, Bob Edwards, Bob Weedon, Michael Engel, Betty Kendall, Mr & Mrs Cubby Broccoli, Russell Turner, Valerie & Sidney James, May & Arthur Askey, The Shadows, Norrie & Joan Paramour, Bob Dawson, Maureen Cleave, Jonah Barrington, June Harris, Dave Paramour, Keith Goodwin, L.G.Wood, The King Brothers, Charles Wintour, Vicky, Nona & Johnny Johnson, Johnny Moran, Sean Kenny, Mr & Mrs Geoff Love, Les Cocks, Rose & Joe Mudele, Mr & Mrs Gary Miller, Michael McGrath, Marion Ryan, Larry Parnes, Don Short, Anna Quayle, Mildred & Victor Ledger, Eric Carter, Mike Nevard, Barry Kingston, Linda & Rex North, Richard Sear, Eric Linden, Tom Merrin, Johnny Franz & Leslie Gould, Terry O'Neill, Mick Jagger, Roy Castle, Peter Carver, Rod Harrod, Winnie Cliff, Cousin Ivor, ReneFreeman, Michael Silver, Claus Voorman, Dickie Leeman, Brian Sears, David Brown, Howard French, Peter Jones, Norman Burns, Penny Valentine, Alan Wilton, Carlos del Rico del Mazo, Pearl & Clifford Davis, Britt & Peter Sellers, Emile Littler, Mr Kawasaki, Sal Chianti, Hugh Mendl, Tony Hancock, Jack Bentley, Sid Green, Frankie Howerd, Ray Orchard, Alan Gabriel, Harry Towb, Beryl & Derek Franklyn, Arthur Haynes, Harold Miller, Jack Parnell, Neville Martin, Anne Shelton, Mr & Mrs Silverstone, Jack Train, Norman Wisdom, Edith Teague, Sam Wanamaker, Peter Dacre, Collie Knox, Ian Ralfini, Gerald Marks, Terry Stamp, Sid Colin, Francis Essex, Bill Prince, Mr Strauss, John T.Frank, Artur Kaps, George Harrison,

Mr & Mrs Phil Goldfarb, Dan Fisher, Ted Ashley, Mitch Halperin, Winnie & Lou Levisohn, Arthur Lewis, Yvonne & Leslie Bricusse, Dirk Bogarde, Burt Bacharach, Trumble Barton, Don Black, Bob Crewe, Maisie & Harold Fielding, Frank Blaine, Alvin Bennett, Judith Simon, Bill Dana, Eddie Curness, Bill Crozier, Alice & Jerry Dawson, Andy Gray, Harold Davison, Peter Murray, Brian Tesler, Kenneth Williams, Terry-Thomas, Andre Previn, Andrew Oldham, Danny la Rue, Paddy Hampshire, Olga Franklin, Jo & Michael Carreras, Mary & Jack Benny, Betty & David Lewin, David Nixon, Rico Dajou, Mr Cansdale , Robin Douglas-Home, Dennis Lyons, Biogio, Frank Muir, Frank Lee, Enid Kenmare, Reggie & Nymie Libson, Cliff Richard, Bob Hope, Fenella Fielding, Hugo Keleti, Dave King, Sam Costa, Joan Littlewood, Martin Balsam, Dr Exner, Bob Skaff, Brian Morris, Judy & Tony Reese, Arthur & Audrey Fletcher, Carl Foreman, Jack Hutton, Hughie Greene, Sister Genevieve, Benny Hill, Laurence Harvey, Mr & Mrs Geoff Tansley, Kenneth Hume, Percy & Esther Knopp, Alan Dell, Mike Mansfield, Bill Badley, Kathy Kirby, Mr & Mrs Joe Nofal, Malcolm Morris, Elizabeth Arkless, Doria & Jack Block, Dusty Springfield, Rollo Gamble, Dick Van Dyke, Sophie Tucker, Norman Banks, Jo Linten, Norman Spencer, Dick van Gelder, Gene Pitney, Felicity Beaurepair, Maurice Woodruff, David Platz, Pat Boone, Lionel Blair, The Andrews Sisters, Jim & Alice Craig, Mum, Barbara Barry, Bernard Spier, Barbara Griggs, Brian Gleason, David Marcus & Norman Levy, Brian Clifford, Peter Lichtwitz, Alex Neve, Rudy Horn, Barry Feinstein, Gerd Vesperman, Sy Marsh, Dennis King, Aino & Tubby Block, Major E.Bar Lev, Edith Yigal Kimchi, John Frank, Chris Beard, John McHugh, Melissa & Robert Sadoff, Riggs O'Hara, Jimmy Saville, Miguel Gonzales Bayo, John Dexter, Bob Trachinger, Mr Sekizawa, John Temple, George Alexander, John Geilgud, Leslie Linder, Richard Armitage, Andy Green, Johnny O'Keefe, Bob Bluett, Chris Hutchins, Barry Dalton, Colin Hopkins, Billy Marsh, Laurence & Joan Olivier, Mel Torme, Mary Arnold, Tony Foreward, Mark Herron, David Gell, Emlyn Williams, Norman Rosewood, Marty Stevens, Liza Minelli, Bill Offner, Lily & Ralph Morris, Michael Caine, Jack Good, Nicola Pietrangeli, Stella & Frankie Vaughan, Willis Hall, Jimmy Booth, Mary & Phil Salimoni, Arnold Baxter, John McDonald, Jack Entratter, Norman Vaughan, Sidmore Parnes, Sheldon Lennard, Tony Benson, Paris Eager, Herbie Wise, Norman Rosemont, Derek Taylor, Matt Monro, Bert Knight, Eddie Jarrett, Peter Ritchard, Rita Tushingham, Michael Slurman, Bruce Welsh, Hank Marvin, Max Judie, Roland Venney, Peter Gormley, Malcolm Lockyer, Fred Sadoff, Bea & Stanley Tollman, Patti Boyd, Evelyn & Sidney Tollman, Harry Rabinowitz, Kathy & Lou Grade, Georgia Brown, Paul Fenhoulet, Helen Noge, Di & Arnold Tollman, John Libson, Cilla Black, Gerry Mander, Howard Koch, Hal David, Johnny Worth, Sandra, Dionne Warwick, Cyril Fletcher, Norma Foster, Roy Parker, Malcolm Goddard, Bev & Jack Hylton, Tommy Cooper, Chuck Berry, Ronnie Hilton, Carl Perkins, Joe Henderson, Sydney, Audrey & Tony Kells, Barry Langford, John Leyton, Tony Lewis, Walter Landauer, Robert Mellin, Ken Dodd, Johnny Franz, Rosemary Squires, Duncan Melvin, Keith Fordyce, Bob Kennedy, Dave Forrester, Derek Chinnery, Brian Matthew, Dr & Mrs Meyer, Joyce & Jules Buck, Robert Nesbitt, John Richards, Joan & Tony Osborne, Leslie MacDonnell, Stan Stern, Philip Ridgeway, Betty & Jimmy Rackley, Joan & Leslie Randall, Dick Richards, Tom Clegg, John McMichael, Jean Carroll, Mr & Mrs Irving Chezar, Peter Charlesworth, Percy Dickins, The Dallas Boys, Pat & Ron Mears, Bob Sharples, Mr & Mrs Jack Solomons, Dorothy Squires, Bill Bourne, Diana Dors, Paul Boyle, Jack Jackson, Roderick Mann, Maureen Cox, John Junor, Frank Lee, Sydney Jacobson, Sheila & Cyril Stapleton, Tom Wiseman, Charles Burt, Peter Wilkinson, John Burgess, Ron White, Ron Randall, Diane & Sean Connery, Glen Mason, Joan Regan, April Young, Mike Winters, Glyn Jones, Bernie Winters, John Junkin, Honor & Maurice Kauffman, Syd Coleman, Ted Brennan, Arthur Lewis, Jimmy Woolf, Jimmy Carreras, Ken Passingham, Ray Coleman, David Nathan, Tommy Trinder, Billy Walker, Bob Holness, Derek Johnson, Gil King, Jimmy Saville, Tony Randall, Nina & Frederick, Alan Tucker, Robin McGill, Judy Lockhart-Smith, Jack Matthews, Toni & Jimmy Dark, Bent Fabric David de Pinner, Lord & Lady Waterpark, Mr Holmstead, Joe Davis, Rene, John Dubois, Ivan Paul, Tom Mboya, Ruth Wallis, Lena & Lennie Heyton, Al Grossman, Bobby Rydell, Helmut Blumgarten, Bob Dylan, Christopher Moore, Lucille Ball & Garry Morton, David Seville, Milton Berle, Mr Radstone, Jack Paar, Pat Johns, Johnny Carson, Joan Anderson, Harvey Risco, David Susskind, Harry Lotzoff, David Merrick, Mark White, Lloyd Shirley, Dr Paul Seidman, Ginette Spanier, Mr & Mrs David Langdon, Norman Hartnell, St John Roper, Vicky Mr & Mrs Kerzner, Jill Kaplan, Feliks Topolski, Emma & Joe Kentridge, Norah & Bernard Docker, Phil Green, Raphael & Leonard, Sid Green, Dick Hills, Alan Blakeley, Sandra & Dick Harmell, Ken Howard, Buorn Lundholm, Arthur Howes, Alice Lee Boatwright, Murray Druker, Ken Hyman, John Bryan, Barry Ferber, George Carden, Dave Dexter, Stanley Donen Camillo, Judy & Alan Carr, John Frank, Eric Merriman, Alan Simpson, Pieter Torien, Ray Galton, Alan Simpson, Davy Kaye, Wilfred Bramble, Richard Hurran, Harry H.Corbett, Ivor Raymonde, David Frost, Steven Vinaver, Danny Williams, Norman Hickman, Ned Sherrin, Janette Scott, Eddie & Bernie Lever, Kim Mills, The Peter Sisters, Michel Engel, Sidney Bernstein, Mr & Mrs Jack Isow, Vince Hill, Dick Shepherd, Robert Menzies...& Michael Joseph

From ALMA COGAN 44 Stafford Court, London W8

of her saying to Michael Caine, while he was helping her to clear up, 'What a nice, tidy boy you are – for an actor.'

Lionel was one of a group of friends who were clearly especially close to Alma during this period. This group also included the actor Stanley Baker, his wife Ellen, Sammy Davis and Mai Britt. It was in Stanley and Ellen's home that Sammy and Mai announced their engagement. That engagement party probably marked the beginning of what Ellen called 'The Great Love Affair', the mutual admiration of

With her good friends Stanley and Ellen Baker.

this group of bright, fun-loving and talented people.

The 'gang' attended nearly every one of Sammy's perform-ances while he was appearing at the Pigalle, their friendship and camaraderie becoming closer all the while. Sammy, even though engaged to Mai, was obviously completely entranced by Alma . . . and he made no secret of it. One evening, at a glittering dinner party at the White Elephant restaurant, with all of us present except Mai, who had flown back to New York to fulfil a commitment, Sammy stood up at the head of the table, and raised his glass to Mum.

'Fay,' he said, 'all I can say is, that if I weren't already spoken for, Alma and I would have the biggest Jewish wedding this town has ever seen.'

Without missing a beat, Mum replied, 'Well Sammy, all I can say is, thank God you're spoken for!'

Sammy was, of course, only occasionally in London, and generally there was just the foursome of Alma, Lionel, Stanley and Ellen. Like myself, Lionel still finds it difficult to talk about the time when he, Alma and the Bakers were a seemingly carefree foursome on the town. Ellen, though, having bravely survived the tragic loss of her beloved Stanley, is able to chat about, and relive with great pleasure, those happy days.

One of the biggest occasions was in September 1964, the opening night of Lionel's new show *Maggie May* – with all the nerves, thrills, excitement and mixture of emotions that always accompany such an occasion. That evening Stanley was miss-ing. He was out of town, filming on location. Ellen, all five feet two of her, looking smashing in Chanel and sporting the latest Vidal Sassoon cut, was to be escorted by the very tall publicist, Theo Cowan, who often accompanied her to important open-ings or charity events when Stanley was absent.

Ellen and Theo, with the Bakers' car and chauffeur, went to pick up Alma, as Ellen remembers. 'Alma looked absolutely stunning! She was tall as a lamp-post anyway, especially in her very high heels, and Stewart (Alma's hairdresser) had added what seemed like several more feet to her height with an enormous, highly lacquered bouffant.

With Lionel Bart for the opening of his musical Maggie May – *the night Noël Coward asked Alma to remove her 'busby'.*

'We arrived at the theatre to be greeted by Lionel, who was to be Alma's escort for this momentous evening. I'm sure he did not even see us, such was his state of nerves. Amidst all the hubbub we tried to take our seats and get settled before the curtain went up – it was late, as it always is on first nights. We had no sooner achieved a reasonable degree of comfort than Alma felt a tap on her shoulder. We then heard the unmistakable clipped tones and rolled r's of the Master himself, Noël Coward: "Madam, would you kindly rrremove your busby." After much laughter and many apologies we began what must have looked like a ridiculous game of musical chairs, our striking appearances only adding to the general hilarity and excitement of the moment.' It was the beginning of what was to be a very warm friendship between Alma and Noël, with the Master becoming a frequent visitor to the flat.

The press never bothered Alma when she was with the Bakers, but Lionel, good friend as he was, was an obvious candidate for gossip. He was then at the height of his success. *Oliver* and *Fings Ain't What They Used to Be* had made him rich and famous. He had bought a vast house in Chelsea with his earnings, in the hope, it was said, of persuading Alma Cogan to share it, so it was hardly surprising that rumours were rife.

On one occasion Alma had to deny very firmly that they were engaged. Speculation subsided, but only for a while. A few months later a journalist spotted her going off 'to Majorca for a holiday on her own'. He also spotted that Lionel Bart caught the same flight, also for a holiday!

Alma herself gave her own twist to this tale in 1964. To Lionel's intense embarrassment, she celebrated Leap Year by proposing to him herself – on *The Eamonn Andrews Show*. 'Like an idiot,' Lionel now recalls, 'I said I'd have to think about it.'

Ironically, we have no pictures of Lionel, Ellen and Stanley and our other friends at Stafford Court. The whole point was that you could come to the flat and not be photographed, whether it was for a party or just for a cup of tea and game of charades. It is perhaps those casual visits that I miss most of all.

So, too, do Alma's friends.

The downstairs doors of Stafford Court were locked at about ten o'clock at night, but if lights were on in the flat friends would throw a coin to hit one of the windows and we would simply drop the keys down so they could let themselves in. The window sills were littered with pennies! To this day Tommy Steele says that whenever he and his sweet wife Annie drive down Kensington High Street, they look up at the flat and ask each other, 'Are the lights still on?'

Right: *Alma was always being photographed in restaurants, and she loved it. I seem to be nervous; I was opening in a new show at the Establishment.*

Opposite: *With Bob Hope. He always asked for Alma to appear with him when he came over to do a show at the Palladium. They got on very well and enjoyed working together.*

A ball at Grosvenor House in aid of mentally handicapped children. Alma is standing between Harry Secombe and Bernard Cribbins, with Joyce Blair, Peter Sellers and David Jacobs at the table.

11

Mrs Macogie Makes Sandwiches

The slinky new look of the 1960s.

S O MUCH has been written about the 'Swinging Sixties' and it seems to me that our flat in Kensington was the hub of it. London was truly the most thrilling place to be at that time. The entertainers, the music, the great clubs and restaurants – we loved every minute of it. And we thought it would last for ever.

Every night, before or after our shows, there would be wonderful get-togethers, conversations and laughs at Mario and Franco's Terrazza or The White Elephant. Alvaro's was great fun on Saturday afternoons, but one of our favourites was the Trattoo, probably because it was right across the street from our flat. Alan Clare played piano in the bar and Pasquale always greeted us like old friends.

I was in a satirical revue at The Establishment in Soho, owned by Peter Cook. The Establishment was an amazing club. Our revue was the regular attraction, but downstairs you could hear some terrific jazz piano from Dudley Moore, and Peter would bring in new British and American entertainers as well. It was the first club in England Lenny Bruce appeared in.

One night Tony Lewis, an agent/manager and good friend, took Mum and Alma to see Lenny Bruce. Lenny was famous for using crude language in his act. 'There I was,' says Tony, 'sitting with Alma and Fay, neither of whom approved of blue language, and there was Lenny Bruce, saying everything in the most graphic terms. I began to feel uncomfortable. I kept glancing at Alma and Fay to get an idea of their reaction, but couldn't.

'When we were outside after the show, I didn't quite know

what to say. Alma broke the silence. "Well, I've never quite seen anything like that," she said. "Nor I," said Fay. Then Alma said, "I think it's time to go home," and I said, "Right, I'll just call a f—ing cab." That broke the tension and they both almost fell down with laughter. Alma and Fay might not like bad language, but there was sure nothing wrong with their sense of humour.'

Whilst working at the Establishment, I would often see a young, good-looking man in the audience. One night he introduced himself and told me how much he enjoyed my work. I asked him what he did. 'I'm with a group,' he said. 'We have a record coming out in a few months.'

I lost touch with him for a time, but when I discovered what his record was I could see why he was busy. It was 'Love Me Do', and his name was Paul McCartney. The Beatles had taken off.

John Lennon and 'Mrs Macogie'. John always preferred to visit us when there was no one else around.

Above: An excerpt from a thirty-page letter from Alma. She talks about Paul and me – I think she was trying to make a match! And here I am with Paul in the flat.

Opposite: Just a few of the regular visitors to our flat . . .

Alma met the Beatles when, just a few months later, after the record came out, they appeared with her on a *Sunday Night at the London Palladium*. She and the boys became instant friends during rehearsals, sharing the same sense of humour. Alma asked them back to the flat after the show. The Beatles, even then, had to be smuggled out of the side door of the theatre in order to avoid the screaming fans. As a result, they arrived at the flat before Alma. Alma hadn't phoned ahead to warn us they were coming. Fortunately, Paul and I already knew each other, so it all worked out, once I'd got over my initial nerves at playing hostess to four Beatles.

There was no one else there that evening, but that was just what they wanted. Those were the early days of Beatlemania, and they needed to relax and get away from crowds. Our flat gave them refuge for many months to come, with Mum – Mrs Macogie, as they called her – making pots of tea and sandwiches, and playing charades. Naturally, most of these gatherings didn't get started until quite late and could run into the wee hours. I remember one night Mum said, 'Ringo, it's 4 a.m. Go home.'

Later, Alma became particularly close to John. His pet name for her was Sara Sequin. But at first we saw rather more of Paul, who would drop into the flat at all hours. One time, with his niece in tow, a lovely little girl, he brought the three of us a gift. It was the biggest bottle of Hermes perfume I've ever seen. It looked like a gallon.

Late one evening Paul was fooling about on our mini piano, and found a melody that caught his fancy. He asked if we had a piece of empty manuscript. I dug one out of the office and he wrote down the tune, humming it as he did so. I thought it was beautiful. It had an unusually haunting and romantic quality to it.

'What are you going to call it?' I asked.

He shrugged.

At that point Mum came in. 'Do you know it's three o'clock?' she said. 'How would you like some scrambled eggs?'

'That's it,' shouted Paul. 'We'll call it "Scrambled Eggs".'

The melody survived. The title did not. It was changed to 'Yesterday'.

Mum said, 'I'm sure it would have done just as well as "Scrambled Eggs".'

It was during the filming of *Antony and Cleopatra* that Alma met Elizabeth Taylor and Richard Burton. She had gone to their hotel with John Heyman, who was their agent at the time. Ironically, Alma had become close friends with Richard's wife Sybil, who would arrive almost every other day through that period of film-making. Alma, Roddy McDowall (who was also in the film) and I would all sit trying to console Sybil about her husband's much publicized romance with Miss Taylor. When she realized her marriage was over, she said, 'I'm moving to New York.'

Her friends had mixed feelings, naturally, and Sybil had many friends. She was a lovely person, but she was determined. Alma arranged a going-away present – a photograph, taken by Roy Round, of as many of Sybil's chums as she could muster. When I was in New York a while later, I went to see Sybil at her disco, Arthur's. It had just opened and was a big success. She was very happy.

'See that gorgeous young man up there?' She pointed to the leader of the rock group who were playing on stage. His name was Jordan Christopher. 'I'm going to marry him,' she said.

Many years later, Sybil and I had lunch in LA, where she was working as a literary agent. She told me about her marriage to Jordan and how happy she was. She also encouraged me to write this book, and I am very grateful to her.

Between her trips overseas and her TV shows, Alma was now also writing several of her own songs with Stan. For the first few songs they used their own names, but after that they liked to use pseudonyms. Alma's favourite was Al Western (from our telephone number, Western 4488) and Stan's was Stephen Forest (an anagram of Stephen Foster). The first of their songs Alma recorded was 'It's You', produced by George Martin, the

Beatles' producer at Columbia. The most successful was probably 'Now That I've Found You', which came from a symphony Stan had written years before he met Alma. It was produced by the Rolling Stones' producer Andrew Loog Oldham, and she also recorded it in German.

One night, Alma went to a club out of London to hear a new singer. She came home raving about him. 'He's incredible,' she enthused. 'What a voice . . . and he's head to toe in black leather! He's going to be a big star.' It was Tom Jones.

Alma told Stan that they must write a song for him. Tom

The photo of Sybil Burton's friends that Alma organized as a farewell present when Sybil went to New York.

With her recording manager from EMI, Norman Newell.

Above: *Alma learning to sing in Japanese, with one of the voice coaches sent over by the Embassy.*

Opposit: *On stage at the Talk of the Town.*

came to the flat to hear it. He was very different from what I had imagined – quiet and soft spoken. He loved the song and wanted to make it the B side of his new single, 'It's Not Unusual'. Stan said, 'No, it's too good a song to be a B side.'

Alma said, 'Stan, half of something is better than a hundred per cent of nothing.' But Stan won that argument and a few months later, when the record was selling in the millions, Stan said, 'That was the dumbest decision I ever made.'

It was about this time that Alma began to feel that the public was losing its taste for novelty songs. She hadn't had a best-selling record for a while and was anxious to develop some new material in order to keep up with the fast-changing times. Wally Ridley did not agree. He believed they had a successful formula and it wouldn't make sense to change. Still, when the break with Wally finally came, he accepted it gracefully. They had had ten years of success, but now it was time for Alma to move on.

There were three other producers at EMI. One of them was Norman Newell. He was already a close friend and Alma had always been impressed with his work. She told him what she had in mind and asked him to be her producer. Alma recorded a lot of wonderful songs with Norman. One of her favourites was one he wrote especially for her, with Cyril Ornadel: 'With You in Mind'. It became the title song for one of her albums.

Norman also discovered a song called 'Cowboy Jimmy Joe' in Germany. He wrote English lyrics for it, Alma recorded it and they had a hit. Now that Alma was so big in Japan, they decided to translate it yet again, this time into Japanese.

'Alma, perfectionist as she was,' Norman remembers, 'called the Japanese Embassy, and asked if they would send some-one over to help her with the pronunciation. Well, they sent three men. They sat in the recording booth, and they would nod their heads up and down for "No good" and shake their heads back and forth for "Good". It was hysterical – there was I, supposedly a big EMI record producer, and Alma, a major star, singing my song – and these three little men had taken over the recording.'

Most of Alma's income in those hectic years came from TV and from her overseas record sales and tours. Variety tours in Britain were, of course, still worth the effort when she could fit them in, but she now earned far less from British record sales. This was true for most girl singers in the 1960s, although the British groups were now doing wonderfully well. Led first by Cliff Richard and the Shadows and then by the Beatles, they had driven the US groups off the top of the British charts.

Naturally Alma felt badly when her records failed to make the charts – but she never allowed herself to dwell on disappointment. Besides, Robert Nesbit and Bernard Delfont had asked her to star at their new, and very prestigious, Talk of the Town, which they had created out of the London Hippodrome. On her opening night, Robert said to her, 'Well, here you are, right back where you started.'

It was one of the most important nights of her life – a gala, star-studded evening, with all her friends there to support her. She designed a wonderful dress of ostrich feathers and chain mail. I remember it weighed seven pounds. Again she had material specially written for her, and this time she and I wrote a parody sending up the Beatles. They loved it.

'Alma Cogan, I hate you, you are so good.'

Those were the words Ethel Merman said to Alma when she came backstage after the last performance of Alma's three-week engagement at Talk of the Town. It had been hugely successful. Miss Merman was opening there the following Monday, and she had come to see Alma's show.

When the two met, there was instant mutual admiration. Alma told Ethel she would like to give a party for her, to welcome her to London. La Merman, in that familiar voice like a trombone solo, said, 'Sure I'll come, honey, but on one condition – I wanna meet the Beatles.'

That presented no problem, but Alma was determined that this was to be the party to top all parties. She began arranging things with her usual enthusiasm, sending out the word that it would be the event of a lifetime. Everyone who was anyone

wanted to be there and, I think, except for those who were out
on tour, they all made it. It was quite a gathering. The guest list
read like a *Who's Who* of show business, and the crush of
performers at the piano was like opening day at Harrods sale.
Miss Merman was in rare form, swapping stories with Alma
and Noël Coward, but even she had to admit that, in London,
Alma was 'the hostess with the mostest'.

At one point, I was sitting in the dining room with my
mother and George Harrison. My mother was, as usual, wearing dark glasses and smoking a long black cheroot. 'Do you
know that Noël Coward is in the other room?' she said to
George.

With a straight face and his best Liverpudlian accent, George
responded, 'Who's he?'

Meanwhile, Paul sat at the feet of the Master, soaking up
every word. 'Young man,' said Coward to McCartney, 'be
satirical.'

Food and supplies were being delivered all evening. My
mother was famous for her *bons mots*, and that night featured
one of her best. The doorbell rang; she, assuming it was yet
another delivery, opened the door to a tall man wearing a long
coat and a beret. Not giving the man a chance to speak, she
said, 'Ice around the back, please,' and closed the door in his
face. A few moments later the doorbell rang again. This time I
opened the door and realized it was Chuck Berry. He thought
Mum was hilarious.

That party was not only our best; it also attracted the most
attention, both from the press and from our neighbours. We
must have had the most patient and long-suffering neighbours
in London. They certainly suffered that evening, and in the
early hours Alma found herself apologizing profusely to one
irate gentleman in pink pyjamas. The problem was not with
our guests, who were careful to keep the noise within bounds,
but with the Beatles' and Rolling Stones' fans. They had discovered where their heroes were, found their way past the
porters and invaded the landing outside the flat.

That was not the only problem, though. Stanley Baker spotted a microphone swinging to and fro outside the window. Reaching through the window, he cut it free and impounded it. We were being bugged. The kids from the flat above were after some original Beatles and Stones conversation. They could hardly be blamed. When, ever again, would there be the opportunity to eavesdrop on a singalong featuring the likes of Mick Jagger, Keith Richard, Chuck Berry, Paul McCartney and Cliff Richard?

Somehow, during the next few days, the press heard about the party and had a field day with the story. They blew up, out of all proportion, the 'disturbance of the peace', and they loved the bit about the aborted microphone. They also discovered that we'd had a fortune teller there and that the celebrities were queuing outside my bedroom, where Mabel was set up, to pay a pound to have their palms read. It was, however, all written about with good humour.

The press coverage detailed who else was there that evening. In addition to those I have mentioned, they listed: Max Bygraves, Bobby Vee, Gene Pitney, Bruce Forsyth, Brian Epstein, Roger Moore, Peter and Mary Noble, Terry and Tito Burns, Paddy and Alfred Marks and Mr and Mrs Bernard Delfont. I'm sure I've missed some names because, in addition to performers, actors and musicians, Alma numbered among her friends politicians and titled folk, having met so many through her work with various charities.

That night remains in my mind exactly as Alma predicted: the event of a lifetime.

As far as many of our famous guests were concerned, one of the attractions of our parties was that we didn't take photographs. So this press photo of Alma clearing up next day is all we have to show of the great Ethel Merman party.

Through John, Paul, George and Ringo, we also naturally met their manager, Brian Epstein. Immediately the press spotted him as another candidate for Alma's hand. So did Mum. He fitted the bill as far as she was concerned. He was a gentleman, good-looking, well educated and Jewish – a mother's dream come true. However, although he and Alma were very fond of each other, there was never any more to their relationship than that.

Brian was already proving himself one of the best managers

in show business, but he was basically a shy person and often seemed at a loss in a big party. He was most at ease, we found, having tea in the flat when there was no one else around but us, or taking Alma out for a quiet meal where they could talk over work or personal problems.

In 1964, Alma gave a press interview, saying, 'The man I marry would have to be interested in my career. He would have to understand what it means to me. He would have to put up with rehearsals, with tours and with times that take no account of normal working hours.' The chances of finding someone she could love and who could fulfil these requirements seemed slim – until she met another Brian.

Alma had in fact first met Brian Morris briefly some years earlier. I had introduced them. I was working at the Stork Club, which was owned by Al Burnett. Brian was Al's nephew, and was working at Les Ambassadeurs. He would finish work, come over and stand at the back of the Stork Club watching the show. Much to his annoyance, he was always introduced to everyone as 'Al Burnett's nephew'.

When he and Alma next met, Brian was very much his own man. He had his own club by then, the Ad Lib. It was a disco and restaurant in Leicester Square, on top of the Prince Charles Theatre, and unique in many ways. They served all the drinks in miniature bottles, the disc jockey wore a dinner jacket and kept his equipment in a piano. The atmosphere set a new trend in private clubs and the Ad Lib became the most popular place of the 1960s. This was due mostly to Brian's flair and his experience at Les Ambassadeurs, but Brian always claims that I played a key part in its success.

'For the first two or three weeks the club wasn't doing too well. Then one night Sandra brought in George Harrison and John Junkin. George loved it and a few nights later he brought Ringo. In 1964, to have one Beatle on the premises was something. To have two Beatles in one night was incredible. The news went through town like wildfire.

'We found we had 300 customers packed shoulder to shoulder every night. We decided they needed exercise. We had hired a cook who could play the tambourine and a waiter who was a great dancer. At given moments, when the place was jammed, the cook came out with his tambourine, the waiter downed his tray and they led everyone off in a conga up and down the stairs, through the bar and in and out of the kitchen.'

Knowing she would love it, I told Alma about the Ad Lib, and Alma took Judy Garland and Dirk Bogarde. She was introduced to Brian – this time by his proper name – and Brian gave Alma her very own table that was always available to her – 'Just inside the door as you come in on the right,' she would tell her friends.

One thing led to another. She and Brian went out to supper, found they shared the same interests and most importantly, as Brian recalls, the same sense of humour. 'What we liked about each other were very simple things. We laughed a lot together. I loved the way Alma noticed things others missed: an absurdly elaborate decoration on a cake, a beautiful spray of flowers almost out of sight upon a pillar. Most people never seem to see anything above eye level, but not Alma. She would always notice things like that, and comment in mock heroic tones, "I don't think we are ready for anything quite so exquisite, are we?"'

She in turn enjoyed Brian's obvious interest in her work and his practical approach to the world of show business. He under-stood that success required business sense as well as talent, and was refreshingly unbedazzled by her reputation. For the last ten years he had been working every night and hardly ever watched television. He knew she was successful, but had little idea of quite how well known she was to the general public, until he casually told his mother that he was going out with Alma Cogan.

'*Alma Cogan?*' Mrs Morris was thrilled. 'I have nothing to wear for the wedding.'

By then Brian had discovered that it was impossible to go out with Alma unnoticed. She was also, of course, very busy. It was not easy for Brian to have a girlfriend who was apt to say

Dresses weren't the only item of clothing Alma cared about – she had a lot of fun with hats, too. The hat on the left was being tried on by Elizabeth Taylor when Alma first saw it. 'No, dear, you need to be taller to wear that,' Alma said, and promptly bought it herself.

that she could not keep a date, because she was off next week to Australia. Still, Brian was ambitious, too, and just as serious about his work. They matched each other well.

I was then at the Mermaid Theatre in *The Royal Commission Review*, directed by Spike Milligan. Alma and Brian had come to the first night and I saw a lot of them throughout 1964. At this time some of Alma's closest friends were beginning to feel a little hurt. They would repeatedly ring the flat with plans for various parties, only to find that Alma was out somewhere with Brian, very often with Ringo and and his girlfriend Maureen. The four had become close friends. It seemed to the others that Brian was taking up what little spare time Alma had.

And yet Brian found that he, too, had limited claims on Alma's time. One day he arrived at the flat to take her out. She was on the telephone. She stayed on the telephone without a break for the next two hours.

'What on earth have you been talking about?' he stormed. 'Nothing is worth two hours on the telephone.'

'Yes, it is,' she said. 'That was Lionel Bart. His show is in trouble. He needs reassurance.'

Brian also had to accept that John Lennon had a special place in Alma's life and that, like Lionel, he depended very much on her sympathetic ear. John would often pop in to the flat on his way back from the airport, just to see her or play her some new song.

A few years ago when I was in Los Angeles, Albert Goldman called me. At the time he was writing his book on John Lennon. He was quite blunt.

'Did your sister have an affair with John Lennon?' he asked.

He caught me by surprise.

'I don't know,' I said, and I didn't. If I had known, I wouldn't have told him. But what I do know is that they were very close, and I sometimes wonder if they're together somewhere now, having a giggle at all of us.

12

Yesterday

IN 1965 the Ad Lib burned down and Brian found another place in Covent Garden. Without telling Brian, Alma asked John if the Beatles would play at the opening. John was immediately enthusiastic and started making plans, but then the deal for the new club fell through. Brian, for the first time in twelve years, found himself with time heavy on his hands.

'Look,' Alma said, 'you are not doing anything. Why don't you come on tour with me?'

With the members of a band who toured with her in Sweden.

On tour in Sweden, 1964.

Contacts taken by our cousin Howard Grey who, like his father, had become a professional photographer.

The tour was round clubs in the north of England. For Brian it was a revelation. He had, of course, seen Alma on stage in London and in the studio. But this was very different. It was Alma in her element. Here was more than admiration. It was true affection of the kind she had first seen expressed for Gracie Fields back in 1955. Now, ten years on, Alma felt it for herself.

Next, she took Brian off to Majorca for a night-club engagement, and then on to Germany. This was a different world again. Here she was an international star come to make a record for the German office of EMI especially for her German fans. Alma enjoyed working in Germany. She even recorded in German, and the fans loved it.

'Tennessee Waltz' had topped the Beatles in the charts for three months in Sweden. In Germany it became a number one hit and sold 350,000 copies.

By the time Alma and Brian returned to England, I was leaving on my own travels. In February 1965 Ned Sherrin and David Frost had asked me to do the US tour of *That Was the Week That Was* with Willie Rushton and Al Mancini, taking over from Millicent Martin.

I was delighted to be back in America with such a prestigious show, and the weekly phone calls were long and newsy. I dread to think of the phone bills, as I reversed the charges – well, you try making a transatlantic call from Kankakee, Illinois. The most exciting news was that Alma and Brian were engaged, unofficially as yet, but yes, definitely planning to get married.

Some pray to marry the man they love,
My prayer will somewhat vary,
I humbly pray to heaven above
That I love the man I marry.

Alma once quoted these words to describe her attitude to marriage. It seemed that at last she had found him.

There had been rumours of romance in the press as early as March that year. When Alma had come back hurriedly from an engagement in Stafford feeling ill, she had been met by a visibly concerned Brian, and she had to go into the usual routine of describing him as a 'good friend'. Since then interest had died down and now, as they kept the news of their engagement to the family and close friends, and always would, the press did not pursue them further.

Journalists had accepted that, when it came to her personal life, Alma was a very private person, and she always gave them such good copy on her latest professional activities that they saw no need to investigate her domestic plans too closely. That October, for instance, she gave them a field day. They had both Alma and the Beatles in the same headline, as Alma went off to Abbey Road to record five songs composed by John Lennon and Paul McCartney. Actually she wanted to do a whole album of their songs, but her producer was against it. I've always thought it would have been a terrific idea.

John and Paul attended the recordings and were 'knocked out' by Alma's big-ballad interpretation of 'Eight Days a Week'. It shot into the charts. Backed by 'Help', it was the last single to be released in her lifetime.

At that time, I was in Chicago, appearing in Second City, an improvisational night club, and wanted Mum to come and join me. My engagement was turning into a very long and successful one. I really enjoyed the improvising; it gave me a chance to write on my feet. To tempt her, I told Mum that Chicago was no distance from Las Vegas. I knew she would love that.

'Sorry, dear,' Mum said, 'Alma has to have minor surgery – nothing serious – something to do with her appendix.'

'How soon?' I asked.

'It looks like February. The doctor wants her to take a fortnight off. She's fine. Don't worry. Anyway, Brian is moving into the flat. So he can keep me company.'

Brian's moving into the flat? I did not know what to worry about more – Alma or Mum. Her calm acceptance of Brian moving in was entirely out of character. Alma and Brian must have been working miracles if they had got her to accept that without protest.

Still, apparently all went according to plan and when Alma

1964: Alma and Lionel Bart taking Christmas to St Giles in the Fields, in another charity effort in aid of needy children.

went into the clinic, Brian went with her and Mum stayed at home waiting. Brian would telephone with news.

The news, when it came, however, was so devastating that it was not passed on to her, nor to me.

When the doctor came down after the operation, Brian led off cheerfully. 'Just routine, I suppose?'

'No. We found something, and we are very concerned about it.' The doctor was quite explicit. It was cancer.

Poor Brian was shattered. He had had no suspicion and now he had to decide what to do.

The doctor tried to help him. 'We've got most of it and she could well be fine now.' Grasping at that straw of hope, Brian decided that the fewer people who knew the truth, the less the chance of Alma learning of the danger she was in.

When Brian spoke to Mum, he was reassuring. 'Nothing to worry about,' he said. 'Apparently her system *was* infected by a grumbling appendix. They will keep her in for a little to sort her out. I'll tell the press.'

Mum, I am sure, guessed it was not as simple as that, but she decided to go along with what Brian suggested.

Alma certainly had no idea of how ill she was. If she had known, she would have thrown everything into finding the right treatment. Alma never sat back and left things to chance; she battled. Clearly she thought everything was now fine. She felt weak, certainly, but that would soon pass. Meanwhile, why not have a party to cheer everyone up?

Alma did not have just one party, but a series of them over the next few days, as her friends streamed in to see her. The staff had never seen anything like it: there were Harry Secombe, Benny Hill, Eric Morecambe.

Then she was released – perhaps to give the clinic and herself a rest. Alma was met as always by the press, smiled, gave a brief comment and was off back to the flat. Brian bought a cake and they had a bit of a celebration, then she and Brian went off to the synagogue together to give thanks for her return.

It was then that Alma started to talk about making their engagement public. The Royal Garden Hotel in Kensington had just opened, and they had asked her if she would give a party there. 'Let's do that,' she said, 'for the announcement of our engagement.'

Benny Hill recalls that he was walking near Harrods one day, 'when she spotted me from the back of a chauffeur-driven car. She had the driver pull over and offered me a lift. She was out organizing a party for someone, of course. I was a bit shaken by her appearance, though. She had looked fine when I saw her in hospital, but now I saw she had become really thin. It was the last time I saw her.'

Alma was then still under orders to be in bed by ten o'clock each evening. That, for Alma, was like asking her to go to bed at midday. Tommy Steele had just come back from working on

Brian takes Alma home from the Harley Street nursing home after her operation, March 1966.

Broadway and was appalled that she had not let them know she had been ill.

'I'm not really ill,' she said. 'If you come round at eight we can have a rave-up for a couple of hours before I go to bed.'

As she got stronger the parties grew longer too. It seemed she really was on the mend. She called her old friend Jimmy Henney and said he must come to dinner. 'I'm cooking,' she said.

'That in itself was funny,' he recalls. 'She *never* cooked. It sounded like a gag, so old Bill Cotton, Ronnie Carroll and I went up to the flat, and sure enough we had a lovely meal. It was chicken, I think. Fay insisted that Alma had cooked it. We talked and laughed and had a good time, as always. When we left, though, and went downstairs, we felt sad. "Our Alm" was not looking too well.'

She went back to work. In July she recorded *International Cabaret*. It was her last TV show.

'She was her normal, happy self,' said the producer, Stewart Morris. 'She was laughing and giggling all day at rehearsals.'

Yet she was not really as strong as she should have been. She started work on a new album, with the orchestra in the very studio in which she had first sung to Wally Ridley. In fact, she was feeling so weak that she asked to have the orchestra record all the music, so she could come back on a day when she felt stronger and add her voice.

This weakness Alma simply attributed to a slow recovery from her operation. At that time, by an extraordinary twist of circumstances, she was far more worried about me than I was about her. I had fallen ill myself.

In America, I was not too concerned about Alma, having heard that the 'minor surgery' at the clinic had gone well, and I had been concentrating on my own career. The improvised theatre show had transferred from Chicago to New York. It was very exciting, my dream come true. Then in August I collapsed with pneumonia. When I telephoned from the hospital, Alma became hysterical and insisted that Mum catch the next plane to look after me.

So, while Mum supervised my convalescence, Alma determinedly pushed ahead with her commitments. She had been
invited to Sweden and had promised to do a tour there in
August. Not only did she want to start earning again, but as
always she was driven by the need to get her career back on the
road.

Brian went with her, along with a backing group of four
Swedish musicians and a road manager, all in one enormous
American car. The tour was for four weeks, well organized,

Left and facing page 186: *On
stage in Sweden during her last
tour, 1966.*

with good accommodation, but extremely exhausting even for a fully fit performer. All the shows were in amusement parks, in the open air. The stages were small, made of concrete, and the audiences vast.

Somehow she finished the tour. Then when they reached their last hotel, she said quite simply, 'I don't feel well,' and passed out. Brian ordered an ambulance and she was rushed over to the hospital. Next morning the doctor called Brian to one side and said, 'You must get in touch with your doctor in England.'

Brian telephoned Alma's doctor.

'Bring her straight home,' he said.

BEA agreed to fly her back immediately, removing a couple of seats to accommodate the stretcher. She went back to the flat for one last time and the next day went into the Middlesex

Alma and Brian in Sweden, 1966.

Hospital. There she was put in the care of the Queen's personal surgeon, Mr Pinkus.

Brian immediately telephoned us in New York and said that Alma was in hospital. He did not want to tell Mum just how ill she was, but Mum needed no convincing that she should go home.

Meanwhile, still unaware of how grave the situation was, I was doing my best to get fully fit in time to appear on *The Merv Griffin Show*. They had seen me in Second City and this was, for me, an opportunity almost as important as that invitation to appear on *The Ed Sullivan Show* had been for Alma ten years before.

Once back in England, Mum telephoned and suggested that I too should come home. She sounded worried, but was vague about what was wrong. As there was no urgency about her suggestion, I said I would come back directly after the TV show. Then Brian rang and for the first time I realized that something was very wrong indeed. I cancelled my appearance on the show and took the next plane back.

When I arrived in London I went straight to the Middlesex Hospital. The waiting room was overflowing with family and friends. I'd not seen any of them for over a year. I ran to Mum, who was standing with Ivor, Lolita and my nephew Mark, then went immediately up to see Alma. She was heavily sedated but seemed to know me. I sat and we held hands. I decided I must not break down. I must behave as Alma would have . . . and *do* something.

In desperation, I went home and rang Danny Kaye. He was a trustee of the Mayo Clinic and I thought he might know of someone who could help. At that late stage, he wasn't able to offer anything other than comforting words.

The following days were a blur. Mum and I shuttled back and forth between Stafford Court and the hospital. We visited a revered rabbi. Someone even sent in a faith healer. At times like that, one tries everything.

Three weeks from the day she entered hospital, Alma died peacefully on 26 October 1966. She was thirty-four.

Two weeks after the funeral, which was at the Bushey Cemetery in North London, EMI asked me to come to the studio and choose the tracks for the album that Alma had been in the middle of recording. At first I refused – I couldn't bear the idea. Then I thought that even though she had been ill at the time, Alma had worked very hard on the album; she would have wanted it to be released, and someone she trusted to finish selecting the tracks.

Stan had to make some changes in the accompaniment, so he and the orchestra gathered in Studio One at Abbey Road. Stan told me, 'It was one of the most moving experiences of my life. To be conducting that group of hardened professional musicians, playing their hearts out, tears streaming down their faces while they heard Alma's voice coming from the empty booth.'

When Stan was satisfied with the music, I went to the studio and did my best to be objective in completing the album. I wanted to make it one that Alma would have been proud of. It was one of the most difficult things I've ever had to do, to sit there alone, listening to her voice, so soon after she was gone . . . especially the track of 'Yesterday'. I was so deeply affected by that afternoon in 1966 that I couldn't listen to any of Alma's records for at least twenty years afterwards.

But somehow the album got finished and released. It was called *Alma*.

Epilogue

IN collecting material, I have discovered the enormous effect Alma had on her friends. Ellen Baker says, 'Alma changed our lives. She made Stanley and me go out virtually every night; we never would have done it without her. We would be sitting at home and the phone would ring; it would be Alma, with news of a party or performance: "You've got to come, you've simply got to, it's going to be wonderful." We would race upstairs, change our clothes and off we would go – and wind up back at the flat with Fay at four in the morning.' When Alma died there were many people whose lives were changed for ever.

Frankie Howerd told me, 'Alma was instrumental in reviving my career in the early '60s. I was going through a very bad time – I couldn't find any work, I was ready to give up completely, I was filled with despair – when out of the blue, Leslie Grade called me and said Alma wanted me on her TV show, *Startime*. It was very kind of her; it gave me a big boost. We worked so well together. I went on from her show to making my comeback.'

Max Bygraves has an uncanny memory of Alma. He had dinner with her after a show of his and was talking about his hit song 'You Need Hands': 'Alma said, "Let me read your palm, Max, I'm good at it, you know." I gave her my hand and she said, "Just look at all your lines, Max, you see these three lines that go everywhere? You'll live to be a ripe old age." So I said, "What about yours?" She opened her hand and there were just two very clear lines. She laughed and said, "Well, I won't be here next year." I've never forgotten that night.'

Shortly before he died, I interviewed Sammy Davis for television and he talked about Alma. 'She was one of the dearest friends I ever had in my life. She was so kind and helpful when I first came to London. I'd ask her for a personal critique on things; she was my guiding light. When she died, I was devastated. There are certain people you never think of in terms of not being there – they are so vital, literally so alive. She could just light up a room by entering it; she created a party just by being there. She glowed in life. She made people feel good: whether performing or as personal friends, they felt all the better for being with her. It rarely happens in our business – it happens very rarely in life. She was my friend.'

Bob Monkhouse remembers, 'As soon as Alma came into your life, you began to need her. When she was absent, you felt the lack of her – her compassion, her radiance, her loveliness, her fun. She attracted friends as she attracted her audiences, through the sheer force of a personality that made everybody feel better than they had before.

'Once, at the Wood Green Empire, I was angry because the orchestra played my novelty song too fast and I fluffed the words. Alma hated seeing anyone being angry, so she told me not to be so silly and gave me a kiss. I felt better immediately.

'Still, one thing makes me helplessly angry about Alma's death. I think she was robbed. And I think we were robbed too. If she were able to read that, she'd tell me not to be so silly and give me a kiss. That's what I meant earlier on. I still need her.

'I'm happy for these youngsters discovering Alma on CDs. I saw some a few days ago in Our Price in Milton Keynes – a bunch of teens vying with one another to sing the words to "Dreamboat".'

One of the first people I called when I went to live in Los Angeles after Alma died was Danny Kaye. That familiar voice came on the phone: 'Sandra! I'm just leaving for Singapore . . . Come over immediately! I'll change my flight – I'll make lunch.' Half an hour later we were sitting in Danny's kitchen in Beverly Hills. 'I'll never forget her,' he said, 'never.' And he cried.

'This is not the occasion for regrets,' says our friend Michael Joseph. 'It's tempting to say we miss her, but we can console ourselves with the knowledge that a quarter of a century after she left us, she's still here with us – and always will be – singing, chuckling and flinging stardust in our eyes. "She Shall Have Music Wherever She Goes".'

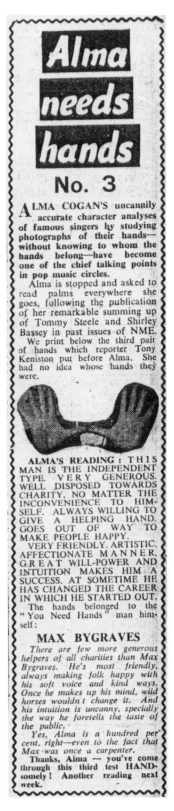

Alma needs hands

No. 3

ALMA COGAN'S uncannily accurate character analyses of famous singers by studying photographs of their hands—without knowing to whom the hands belong—have become one of the chief talking points in pop music circles.

Alma is stopped and asked to read palms everywhere she goes, following the publication of her remarkable summing up of Tommy Steele and Shirley Bassey in past issues of NME.

We print below the third pair of hands which reporter Tony Keniston put before Alma. She had no idea whose hands they were.

ALMA'S READING : THIS MAN IS THE INDEPENDENT TYPE. VERY GENEROUS. WELL DISPOSED TOWARDS CHARITY, NO MATTER THE INCONVENIENCE TO HIMSELF. ALWAYS WILLING TO GIVE A HELPING HAND. GOES OUT OF WAY TO MAKE PEOPLE HAPPY.

VERY FRIENDLY. ARTISTIC. AFFECTIONATE MANNER. GREAT WILL-POWER AND INTUITION MAKES HIM A SUCCESS. AT SOMETIME HE HAS CHANGED THE CAREER IN WHICH HE STARTED OUT.

The hands belonged to the "You Need Hands" man himself:

MAX BYGRAVES

There are few more generous helpers of all charities than Max Bygraves. He's most friendly, always making folk happy with his soft voice and kind ways. Once he makes up his mind, wild horses wouldn't change it. And his intuition is uncanny, specially the way he foretells the taste of the public.

Yes, Alma is a hundred per cent. right—even to the fact that Max was once a carpenter.

Thanks, Alma — you've come through this third test HANDsomely! Another reading next week.

Discography

HMV BD series
6133 Meet Me on the Corner
6138 If'n (with Denny Dennis)
1294 Sittin' in the Sun

HMV B series
10280 To Be Worthy of You/Would You?
10307 (7M107) To Be Loved by You/Homing Waltz (with Larry Day)
10319 Waltz of Paree/Pretty Bride
10338 Half as Much/Blue Tango
10344 (7M106) I Went to Your Wedding/You Belong to Me
10370 Take Me in Your Arms and Hold Me/Wyoming Lullaby
10449 Till I Waltz Again with You/Happy Valley Sweetheart
10460 If I Had a Penny/Hold Me, Thrill Me, Kiss Me
10464 On the First Warm Day (with Les Howard)/LES HOWARD
10505 Till They've All Gone Home/Hug Me a Hug (with Les Howard)
10530 If I Had a Golden Umbrella/Mystery St
10590 My Love, My Love/Wasted Tears
10601 (7M166) Over and Over Again/Isn't Life Wonderful (both with Les Howard)
10615 (7M173) The Moon Is Blue/Ricochet
10653 (7M188) Love Me Again/Bell Bottom Blues
10677 (7M196) Said the Little Moment/Make Love to Me
10698 (7M219) Little Shoemaker/Chiqui Chaqui
10712 (7M226) Do, Do, Do, Do, Do, Do It Again/Jilted (with Frankie Vaughan)
10717 (7M228) Little Things Mean a Lot/Canoodlin' Rag
10743 (7M239) What Am I Gonna Do, Ma?/Skinnie Minnie (Fishtail)
10761 (7M269) This Ole House/Skokiaan
10786 (7M271) Christmas Cards/I Can't Tell a Waltz from a Tango
10802 (Don't Let the) Kiddygeddin/Mrs Santa Claus
10828 (7M286) Paper Kisses/Softly Softly
10832 Mambo Italiano/The Naughty Lady of Shady Lane
10848 (7M301) Tweedle Dee/More Than Ever Now
10862 (7M293) Tika Tika Tok/Chee Chee oo Chee
10872 Dreamboat/The Irish Mambo
10887 Keep Me in Mind/Where Will the Baby's Dimple Be?
10896 (7M316) Give a Fool a Chance/Got 'n Idea
10917 The Banjo's Back in Town/Go On By
10929 Hernando's Hideaway/Blue Again

HMV POP series
129 (7M337) Never Do a Tango with an Eskimo/Twenty Tiny Fingers
163 (7M367) Love and Marriage/The Sycamore Tree
187 Lizzie Borden/Willie Can
189 Bluebell/Don't Ringa da Bell
198 (7M390) It's All Been Done Before (with Ronnie Hilton)/RONNIE HILTON
223 (7M390) The Birds and the Bees/Why Do Fools Fall in Love?
239 Mama, Teach Me to Dance/I'm in Love Again
261 In the Middle of the House/Two Innocent Hearts
284 You, Me and Us/Three Brothers
317 Whatever Lola Wants, Lola gets/Lucky Lips
336 Chantez, Chantez/Funny Funny Funny
367 Summer Love/Fabulous

392 What You've Done to Me/That's Happiness
415 Party Time/Please Mister Brown
433 Love Is/The Story of My Life
450 Getting Ready for Freddy/Sugartime
482 Stairway of Love/Comes Love
500 Fly Away Lovers/Sorry Sorry Sorry
531 There's Never Been a Night/If This Isn't Love
573 Last Night on the Back Porch/Mama Says
608 Pink Shoe Laces/The Universe
670 I Don't Mind Being All Alone/We Got Love
728 O Dio Mio/Dreamtalk
760 The 'I Love You' Bit (with Ocher Nebish)/Train of Love
815 He Just Couldn't Resist Her with Her Pocket Transistor/Must Be Santa
2015 Dreamboat/Twenty Tiny Fingers

Columbia DB series
4607 Cowboy Jimmy Joe/Don't Read the Letter
4679 With You in Mind/Ja-da
4794 She's Got You/In the Shade of the Old Apple Tree
4912 Goodbye Joe/I Can't Give You Anything But Love
4965 Tell Him/Fly Me to the Moon
7059 Hold Your Hand Out, Naughty Boy/Just Once More
7233 I Love You Much Too Much/Tennessee Waltz
7390 It's You/I Knew Right Away
7652 Snakes and Snails/How Many Nights, How Many Nights
7786 Help/Eight Days a Week
8088 Now That I've Found You/More

HMV 7EG series (EP)
8122 Dreamboat/Where Will the Baby's Dimple Be?/Mambo Italiano/Keep Me in Mind
8151 The Banjo's Back in Town/Go On By/Hernando's Hideaway/Blue Again
8169 Lizzie Borden/Willie Can/Bluebell/Don't Ringa da Bell
8532 I Could Have Danced All Night/Wouldn't It Be Loverly?/With a Little Bit of Luck/3 SONGS BY RONNIE HILTON
8437 Life Is Just a Bowl of Cherries/Taking a Chance on Love/Ain't We Got Fun/Blue Skies

HMV CLP series (LP)
1152 I Love to Sing
1459 Oliver

Columbia 33SX series (LP)
1244 Dreamtalk
1345 Alma Sings with You in Mind
1385 The Wakey Wakey Show
1469 How About Love
1635 Tribute to Michael Holliday
6130 Alma

Music For Pleasure MFP series (LP)
1377 The Girl with the Laugh in her Voice
DL1084 With Love in Mind
DL 1191 Almanac
4156431 The Very Best of Alma Cogan

Other LPs/CDs
OU 2168 The Alma Cogan Collection
OU 2213 The Alma Cogan Second Collection
CDMOIR 401 You Belong to Me
CDP 7955942 The Best of the EMI Years
EMI EMS 1280 A Celebration
IMO 4805512 Alma Cogan

Index

Figures in italics refer to picture captions

Ad Lib 170–1, 175
Aida Foster School 26–7
Aladdin 88
Alma 186
Alma Cogan Show 132, 139
Aly Khan, Prince 92
'Amore' 111
And Another Thing 144
Andrews, Archie 41
Anthony, Lily *57*, 77, 96
Aquarium, Brighton 25
Askey, Arthur 64
ATV 78, 88
Atwell, Lou 44, *98*
Atwell, Winifred 43–4, 89, *98*, *99*

Badley, Bill 78
Baker, Ellen 150–2, *150*, 188
Baker, Stanley 148, 150–2, *150*, 167, 188
'Banjo's Back in Town, The' 55
Bart, Lionel 144, *147*, 148–52, *152*, 174, *179*
Basie, Count 71, *100*
Bassey, Shirley 107, 111, 120, 139, 144
BBC 37, 39–41, 44, 52–4, 61, 96, 106
Beatles, The 159–60, 166–8, 170, 175, 178–9
'Begin the Beguine' 13
'Bell Bottom Blues' 34, 53, 86
Belles of St Trinians, The 27
Bennett, Tony 144
Benny, Jack 15, 88
Bentine, Michael 96
Bentley, Dick 39, *40*, 44, 46–7, *47*, 96
Berry, Chuck 167–8
Billy Cotton Band Show, The 106
Billy Liar 148
'Birds and the Bees, The' 89
Black, Michael 147
Blackburn, Bryan 107
Blackpool 19, 64–6, 78, 88, 139
Blair, Joyce 132, *157*
Blair, Lionel 78, 132, *136*, 147
Blue Lamp 28
'Blue Skies' 106
Bluett, Bob 78
Bogarde, Dirk 171
Bricusse, Leslie 6, 12, 147
Bricusse, Yvie 132, 147
Britt, Mai 150–1
Brough, Peter 41
Bruce, Lenny 158
Bruce, Tommy *116*
Burkeman, Lila 147
Burnett, Al 144, 170
Burns, Joe 32, 34–5
Burns, Terry & Tito 168
Burns and Allen 88
Burton, Richard 162
Burton, Sybil 162, *163*
Bygraves, Max 56, *100*, 168, 188, *189*

Café Anglais 28
Caine, Michael 148–50
Calvert, Eddie *99*
Caron, Sandra 11, 14–16, *18*, 20, *21*, 26, *26*, 32, 50, 57–8, *58*, *60*, *64*, 69, 74–5, 105, *105*, 107, 111–14, 138, 142, 144, *147*, 148, *154*, 158, 160, *160*, 170, 174, 178–9, 182, 185
Carp, Gertrude 8, *9*, 21
Carp, Herman, 8, *9*, 21
Carp, Rose 21
Carr, Alan 28–9
Carr, Pearl 139
Carroll, Ronnie 107, 182
Chaplin, Sidney 94
Checker, Chubby 147
Christopher, Jordan 162
Clare, Alan 158
Clark, Petula 58, *110*
Cogan, Fay 7, 8–9, *10*, 11, *12*, 14–16, 18–22, 25, *26*, 35–9, 41, 50, 56–7, 64, *64*, 68–70, 75–6, 105, *105*, 107, 110–12, *114*, *115*, 119, 122, 148, 151, 158–61, *159*, 167, 179, 185, 188
Cogan, Ivor 11, 14, 16, 20, 27, 35, 37–8, 105, *105*, 139–42, 185
Cogan Lolita 139–42, 185
Cogan, Mark (Alma's father) 9–11, *10*, *12*, *13*, 13–16, 18, *18*, 20–2, 25, 30, 34–7, *70*, 75, 87–8
Cogan, Mark (Alma's nephew) 142, 185
Cogan, Sandra *see* Caron, Sandra
Collins, Jackie 118
Collins, Joan 147
Connaught Theatre, Worthing 21, 89
Connery, Sean 148
Conrad, Jess 139
Conway, Russ 139
Cook, Peter 158
Cooper, Tommy 29
Cordell, Frank 37, *40*
Cotton, Bill 107, 182
Cotton, Bill Jnr 34, 53, 107
Coupland, Diana 32
Cowan, Theo 151
Coward, Noël 53, *148*, 152, *152*, 167
'Cowboy Jimmy Joe' 164
Crazy Gang 64
Cribbins, Bernard *157*
Crombie, Josephine *40*
Crooks, Alan 24–5
Cumberland Hotel 32, *32*, 34–6, 41
Cyril Stapleton's BBC Show Band 61

Daiken, Freda 78
Daily Express 74, 116
Daily Mirror 64, 93–4
Dainty, Billy 107
Dallas Boys 107
Dann, Beatrice (née Carp) 8, *9*, 21
Dann, Gerry 21–2
Davis, Clifford 47
Davis, Sammy Jnr 132, 144, 150–1, 188–9

Dawson, Dickie 57–8
Delfont, Bernard 64, 89–92, 166, 168
De Mille, Cecil B. 104
Dexter, John 144
Donegan, Lonnie 100
Donovan, Terence *144*
Don't Lower the Bridge, Raise the Water 138
Dors, Diana 57
Douglas, Paul 94
'Dreamboat' 65, 90, 189
Drew, Larry 111

Eamonn Andrews Show, The 152
Edinburgh, Duke of *62*, 87
Ed Sullivan Show, The 94, 104
Edwards, Jimmy 44, 46–7, *47*
'Eight Days a Week' 179
Elizabeth II, Queen *62*, 64–5, 87, *100*
Elizabeth, the Queen Mother 98
Emery, Dick 29
EMI 164, 178, 186
Epstein, Brian 168–70
Establishment, The 158–9
Everitt, Geoffrey 53

Fields, Gracie 68, *100*
Film Artists' Association 27
Fings Ain't What They Used to Be 152
Finney, Albert 147
Fitzgerald, Ella 71
'Fly Me to the Moon' *124*
Fonda, Henry 94
Fonteyn, Margot *100*
Forces Show, The 41
Formby, George 64
Forsyth, Bruce 88, 168
Foster, Stan 61, 79, 92, 98–100, 102–4, *102*, 107, 120, 130, 134, 138, 162–4, 186
Freeman, Alan *142*, 147
Frinton, Freddie 107
'From This Moment On' 96
Frost, David 178

Gabor, Zsa Zsa 122
Garland, Judy 104, *106*, 132, 144, 147, 171
Garrison Theatre 53
Gates, Jill 77, 78
Gates, Mrs 77, 78
Gently Bentley 39, *40*, 41, 44, 46
Glums, The 47–50
Goldman, Albert 174
Goodman, Derek 122–4, *122*
Goons, The 96
Gordon, Felice 105
Gorme, Eydie 144
Grace, Sidney 43
Grade, Leslie 43, 54–5, *148*, 188
Grade, Lew 43, 94
Grade Agency 43, 107, 132
Graham, Sheilah 118
Grand Theatre, Brighton 22–4, 58
Grant, Betsy 118
Grant, Cary 112–18
Grey, Alf *16*, 79

Grey, Hettie (née Kogin) 8, 9, 19, 79
Grey, Howard, 79, *178*

Hale, Dennis 25
Hammond, Harry *51*
Harrison, George 167, 170
Hawes, Tony 146
'He Just Couldn't Resist Her with Her Pocket Transistor' 128, *130*
Hearne, Richard 43–4
Heath, Ted 19, 53, 64, 71, *99*
'Help' 179
Henderson, Joe 'Mr Piano' 58–60
Henney, Jimmy 107, *107*, 182
Hepburn, Audrey 25, 102
Heyman, John 162
Heyman, Norma 147
High Button Shoes 25–7, 90, 102
Hill, Benny 29, 54, *109*, 117, 180–1
Hiscock, Stewart 79, 151
HMV Records 30–1, 56
Holliday, Judy 94
Hope, Bob *154*
Hopkins, Colin 111–12
Horne, Lena 71, 104
How About Love 144
Howerd, Frankie 139, *141*, 188
Hume, Kenneth 139
Hutton, Betty 144
Hylton, Jack 25, *62*

'I Believe' 56
'I Can't Give You Anything But Love' 122
'I Can't Tell a Waltz from a Tango' 34, 61–4
'If I Had a Golden Umbrella' 44
'If Love Were All' 53
'I'll Make Up for Everything' 22
I Love to Sing 106
'I'm Queen of the Cockneys' 104
'In the Middle of the House' 54, *54*, 89
International Cabaret 182
Isow, Jack 76, 112
ITMA 40
'It's You' 162

Jackson, Jack 37, 39
Jacobs, David 52–3, *142*, *157*
Jagger, Mick 168
James, Graham 111
Jewell, Jimmy 66
Johnson, Teddy 139
Jones, Tom 163
Joseph, Michael *148*, *189*
Juke Box Jury 79
Junkin, John 170

Kavanagh, Ted 40
Kavanagh Productions 40
Kaye, Danny 15, *64*, 66, *66*, 88, 185, 189
Kenmare, Countess of 128
Kidderminster, Sylvia 78
King, Alan 104, *106*
King, Dave 88
Kinn, Berenice 120

Kinn, Maurice 42, 120
Kitchen, The 144
Kitt, Eartha 144
Kogin, Esther (Grandma Cogan) 6, 6–7, 8, *9*, 13
Kogin, Phillip 8, *9*, 13

La Rue, Danny 75
'Last Night on the Back Porch' 110
Laurel, Lois 147
Lawrence, Ivan 21
Lawrence, Leslie 21
Lawrence, Sarah (née Carp) 8, *9*, 21
Lawrence, Steve 144
Lazarus, Bernie 122–4
Lee, Peggy 71, 144
Lennon, John *159*, 160, 174–5, 179
Lewis, Jerry 138
Lewis, Tony 158
Liberace *142*
'Little Shoemaker, The' 58
'Little Things Mean a Lot' 58
'Lobby Song' 66
Lockwood, Sir Joseph 147
London Hippodrome 25, 100, 166
London Palladium 66, 88–9, *142*, 154
London Palladium's Record Star Show, The 89
Luft, Sid *106*
Lynn, Vera 22, 71, 86, *100*, 120, *142*, 144

'Mack the Knife' 124–6
Macmillan, John 41
Maggie May 151, *152*
'Man I Love, The' 19, 25, 30
Manchester Hippodrome 41, 106–7
Mancini, Al 178
Marini, Moreno 111
Marks, Paddy & Alfred 168
Martin, Dean 134, 138
Martin, George 162
Martin, Millicent 178
Masters, Dick 104
Maxwell, Charles 44, 46–7, 50
McCartney, Paul 159–60, *160*, 167–8, 179
McDowell, Roddy 162
Merchant of Venice, The 27
Merman, Ethel 166–7
Merry Macks 62
Merv Griffin Show, The 185
Miller, Max 22, 24
Milligan, Spike 96, 174
Monkhouse, Bob 53–4, *100*, 189

Moore, Dudley 158
Moore, Roger 168
'More Than Ever Now' 84
Morecambe, Eric 54, 107–10, 120, *120*, *148*, 180
Morris, Brian 170–80, *181*, 183, *184*, 185
Morris, Stewart 182
Morris, William 111
'Mr Pastry Comes to Town' 43–4
Muir, Frank 46–7
Murray, Pete *142*
Murray, Ruby 93

'Naughty Lady of Shady Lane, The' 65
Nesbit, Robert 25–6, 64, 89–92, 166
'Never Do a Tango with an Eskimo' 34, 119
New Musical Express (NME) 42, 52–3, 64, 66, *92*, 93–4, 105, 120, 122
Newell, Norman 164, *164*
Newley, Tony 132, 147
Nichols, Joy 44, 46
Noble, Peter & Mary 168
Norden, Denis 46–7, 50
Novak, Sergio 111
'Now That I've Found You' 163

O'Hara, Maureen 74
O'Hara, Riggs 147
Oldham, Andrew Loog 163
Oliver 148, 152
Olivier, Laurence 144
Ornadel, Cyril 164
O'Toole, Peter 147

Pajama Game, The 89
Palace Theatre, Reading 16
Parnell, Val 89
Pasquale 158
Pearl Hood Dancing School 20
Picture Post 96
Pigalle 144–6
Pinkus, Mr 185
Pitney, Gene 168
Plaza Hotel 104–6
'Prisoner of Love' 19

Radio Luxembourg 40, 53, 92–3
Ray, Johnnie *110*
Ray, Raymond 77
Rayne, Robert 118

Ready Steady Go 79
Record Round Up 37
Redgrave, Lynn 75
Regan, Joan 66, 96, 107, 120
Reid, Beryl 90, *91*
Reine, Michael 34
Richard, Cliff *116*, 166, 168
Richard, Keith 168
Ridley, Walter 30–2, 37, *37*, 41–3, 52, 100, 164, 182
Robinson, Cardew 139
Rocking the Town 89–92, *89*, *91*
Rogers, Ginger 104
Rolling Stones 167–8
Roncoroni, Joe 30
Rose, Albert 22
Rose, Clarkson 24
Round, Roy 162
Roy, Harry 28
Royal Commission Review, The 174
Royal Variety Performance 62, 64, 78, 88, *98*, *100*, *141*, *142*
Roza, Lita 42, 93, 96
Ruben, Lee 38
Running Wild 54
Rushton, Willie 178
Ryan, Marion *142*

St Joseph's Convent 14, 16
Sandbach, Sydney 78
Scott, Janette *142*
Secombe, Harry 27, 89–90, *91*, 96, *157*, 180
Secret Keepers, The 139, *141*
Selby's Restaurant 28
Sellers, Peter 96, *157*
Semprini 106
Shelton, Anne 93, *99*, 110, *134*, *142*
Sherrin, Ned 178
Sinatra, Frank 71, 134
Spain, Nancy 71
Speer, Roy 39, *40*
Squires, Rosemary *120*
Stamp, Terence 148
Starr, Ringo 170, 175
Startime 188
Steele, Tommy 146, 148, 154, 181
Stoll Moss Empires 39, 41
Stork Club 107, 111, 144, 168
Straten, Van 19
Sullivan, Ed 94
Sunday Best 106
Sunday Mirror 47
Sunday Night at the London Palladium 88, *99*, 160

'Sussex Queen of Song' 21–2

Take It From Here 44–52, *44*, *47*, 50–2, 54, 122
Talk of the Town *164*, 166
Taylor, Elizabeth 162
'Tell Him' 128
'Tennessee Waltz' 178
That Was the Week That Was 178
Thompson, Kay 94
Thompson, Peter 35
'To Be Worthy of You' 37, *37*, 39–40
Tolman, Stanley & Bea 122
Tormé, Mel 71
Trinder, Tommy 89, 93, *99*
Tucker, Sophie 88
Tushingham, Rita 144
Twinkle 24

Valentine, Dickie 42, 66, *99*
Vaughan, Frankie 71
Vaughan, Norman *142*
Vee, Bobby 168
Veroli, Manilio di 32

Waldman, Ronnie 52
Warris, Ben 66
Watson, Jimmy 37, *37*
Wednesday Startime 78
Weedon, Bert *142*
'We Got Love' 79
'Where Will the Baby's Dimple Be?' 50
Whitfield, David 66, *99*
Whitfield June *44*, 46–7, *47*
'Why Do Fools Fall in Love?' 89
Why the Chicken 148
Widmark, Richard 107
Wilde, Marty *116*
'Willie Can' 89
Wilson, Sandy 111
Windsor Castle 87, 96
Winn, Godfrey 71
Winters, Shelley 147
Wise, Ernie 54, 107, 120, *120*
'With You in Mind' 164
Wood, Fred 71
Wylie Price's Band 21

Yana *142*
'Yesterday' 162, 186
'You, Me and Us' 94
Young, April 40